C

Corsic

In the tumultuous landscape of the Mediterranean, a speck of an island called Corsica danced on the shifting stage of history. It was a place of jagged beauty, with cloud-dappled mountains casting long shadows over verdant valleys and a sun-kissed sea lapping at its rocky shores. Yet, its idyllic aura belied a stormy past. For centuries, this sunburnt Eden was a fiercely contested piece of earth, a pawn in the grand chess game of empires. It was in this world of conflict and contradiction that our protagonist was born.

Born on August 15, 1769, in the town of Ajaccio, Napoleon Bonaparte entered a world on the precipice of dramatic change. His family, the Bonapartes, originally from Tuscany, had embraced their Corsican identity. They were minor nobility and, by the standards of the day, comfortably well-off, but they were far from the opulence and grandeur we often associate with the term 'noble'. They lived in a house, respectable but not grand, with stuccoed walls adorned with family portraits whose eyes seemed to follow you around the room.

As with any epic tale, we must understand the forge in which our hero was shaped, and Corsica was the anvil against which Napoleon's character was hammered. Corsica was an island constantly at odds with itself, split by feuds, vendettas, and fierce clan loyalties. There was a wildness about it, a rugged toughness reflected in its people - and the young Napoleon was no exception. From an early age, he was exposed to the visceral reality of rebellion and resistance. Corsica had, after all, only become a French territory a year before his birth.

Corsica's recent annexation by France followed a long history of turbulent rule by various foreign powers, each leaving an indelible imprint on the island's collective psyche. For Napoleon, this heritage of resistance and rebellion became an integral part of his identity. His awareness of the nuances of power, conflict, and allegiance, born from the crucible of Corsica's fraught history, would influence his future as much as any classroom. The sense of 'us' against 'them' that permeated the very air he breathed was a potent fuel for a mind always questioning, always analyzing.

As he grew older, Napoleon's relationship with his birthplace became more complex. He was a Corsican, proud of his island roots, yet also aware of the broader horizons offered by the French mainland. In the grand scheme of things, Napoleon Bonaparte was not merely a Corsican. Nor was he simply French. He was a man who straddled cultures, identities, and allegiances. It was this cross-cultural background, this unique fusion of island ruggedness and

Napoleon

The life of Napoleon Bonaparte, from humble beginnings to revolutionary, conqueror and Emperor of France

Hourglass History

Table of Contents

continental sophistication, that would shape Napoleon's unique perspective on power, leadership, and statehood.

This Corsican ethos played out in his childhood. He was a boy who showed a strong will, sharp intelligence, and an instinctive grasp of power dynamics. He was proud, stubborn, and unyieldingly ambitious. The Corsican spirit of defiance echoed in his games, which often saw him leading his own army of boys in pretend battles, exhibiting early signs of military brilliance.

We also see in his upbringing, the roots of his complex relationship with women. His mother, Letizia, was a formidable woman of stern beauty and iron will, who kept her brood of eight in line with strict discipline. From her, Napoleon imbibed invaluable lessons of resilience and determination. He would later credit her as being a key influence in his life, saying, "The future destiny of a child is always the work of the mother."

These early years in Corsica, shrouded in the island's violent history and the contradictions of his family's position, laid the foundation for the man Napoleon would become. Yet, as he stood on the cusp of adolescence, the pull of a different world began to beckon. The draw of the French mainland, with its promise of education and advancement, loomed over his future. Corsica had shaped the clay; now it was time for the chisel of France to sculpt the man from the boy.

Yet, the imprint of his Corsican heritage was never far from Napoleon's heart. Even as he rose to conquer much of Europe, his Corsican accent tinged his speech. His strategies reflected the cunning of the island outlaws. His understanding of power and rebellion, nurtured under the Corsican sun, guided his maneuvers on the European stage. The island boy from Ajaccio would transform into a figure larger than life, but the echoes of Corsica would reverberate in the march of his soldiers, in the roll of his cannons, and in the bold strokes of his policies.

In the end, Corsica was more than just the birthplace of Napoleon Bonaparte. It was the canvas on which the first strokes of a grand portrait were painted—a portrait of a boy who would grow to be a revolutionary, a conqueror, and an emperor. A portrait of a man who would forever bear the marks of his Corsican origins.

Chapter 2:

Education in France

In the year of 1778, a ship departed from the rough-hewn coasts of Corsica, cutting through the cobalt blue of the Mediterranean. Among its passengers was a boy of nine years old, swaying gently with the ocean's rhythm, a bittersweet mixture of trepidation and exhilaration written across his face. His name was Napoleon Bonaparte, and he was on a voyage that would take him from the wild landscapes of Corsica to the grand boulevards of France. The island boy was to be transformed into a French gentleman through the crucible of education.

Autun, a small city in eastern France, was Napoleon's first taste of French mainland education. He was enrolled at a religious school run by the Minim friars. Even though his time in Autun was brief—only a few months—it was crucial for his transition. It was here where he began to learn French, the language that would enable him to rise through the ranks of the French army and eventually govern the nation. The child who had arrived speaking a Corsican-inflected Italian was to emerge speaking the King's French.

The boy from Corsica was a foreigner in a strange land, and his struggle to grasp the language, so vastly different from the rustic dialects of his homeland, was not without its challenges. The French he encountered was not just a language but a mode of thinking and expression, a gateway into a world of grand narratives and sublime arts. This difficulty, however, did not deter the young Napoleon. He embraced the language with the tenacity that would come to define his life. It is said he mastered French by sheer determination, spending his nights poring over grammar books and literature, translating passages until he thought in French as naturally as he did in his mother tongue.

In 1779, after mastering the fundamentals of French, Napoleon was transferred to the military school at Brienne-le-Château. The austere routine of a military academy was a world away from the familial warmth of his Corsican home. The students woke at dawn, their days filled with rigorous classes and drills, and lights were out by nine in the evening. It was a regimented life, a dramatic shift for a boy whose free time was spent exploring the rugged landscapes of Corsica. But rather than wilting under this rigid schedule, Napoleon thrived. He was a quick learner and a voracious reader. Among the texts that left an indelible mark on his impressionable mind were Plutarch's 'Lives' and Caesar's 'Commentaries', stirring tales of valor and heroism that would fuel his ambition for greatness.

Despite his academic prowess, Napoleon was not a popular boy. He was often mocked for his Corsican accent and perceived as an outsider. His fellow students, mostly sons of French nobility, saw the island boy as a curiosity, a foreign entity to be examined, not befriended. But Napoleon did not bow to these societal pressures. Instead, he found solace in solitude, using his free time to explore the rich tapestry of history through books. The echoes of great men who shaped history became his companions. They stoked his dreams, fueled his ambitions, and taught him lessons in leadership and statesmanship.

During his time in Brienne, Napoleon's military talents began to manifest. At the academy, students learned the art of warfare, studying the strategies of the great battles and learning the disciplines of artillery, cavalry, and infantry. Here, Napoleon showed a remarkable aptitude for artillery, a branch of the army often considered as the most intellectually demanding. He excelled in mathematics and geometry, subjects vital for the calculations required in artillery warfare. His teachers noted his ability to grasp complex concepts and his keen interest in tactical studies.

A particular incident stands out during his time in Brienne. It was during a snowball fight, a tradition at the academy that was more a mock-battle than a game. The boys were divided into two armies, complete with infantry, cavalry, and fortifications. Napoleon, leading one side, showed strategic brilliance and leadership that belied his age. He marshalled his forces, developed an elaborate battle plan, and eventually won the day. This was a harbinger of the future, a glimpse of the military genius that would change the course of history.

But Napoleon's years at Brienne were more than just a military education. It was also here that he cultivated his fascination with history and philosophy. He devoured books on the French Enlightenment, and the ideas of liberty, equality, and fraternity took root in his mind. He admired the works of Voltaire and Rousseau, reading and rereading their treatises until their thoughts became his. This thirst for knowledge was not limited to books. Napoleon would often engage his teachers in lengthy debates, challenging their ideas and defending his own with passionate eloquence.

After completing his education at Brienne in 1784, Napoleon was admitted to the prestigious École Militaire in Paris. He was just fifteen, but he carried himself with the gravitas of a man. Here, he completed a two-year course in one year, demonstrating an insatiable hunger for learning and an unrivaled determination.

His years at École Militaire were a time of growth and exploration. He was now in the heart of France, surrounded by the echoes of its illustrious past and the whispers of its uncertain future. The institution was a bastion of the French aristocracy, and for the young Corsican, it was a foray into the complexities of class and privilege. These experiences etched deep into his psyche, shaping his views on society, power, and governance.

Napoleon's education in France was far more than a journey of academic learning. It was the shaping of a mind, a mind that would one day hold the fate of Europe in its hands. Through the rigors of military training and the liberating power of intellectual exploration, the Corsican boy was metamorphosed into a French gentleman, equipped with the tools to navigate the intricate tapestry of French society and politics. It was these formative years that laid the foundation upon which the legend of Napoleon Bonaparte was to be built.

Chapter 3:

The Revolutionary

O n the dawn of August 9, 1793, a solitary figure could be seen gazing out into the bay of Toulon. He was a young man of only twenty-four, far removed from the corridors of power in Paris, where the tempest of the French Revolution had ignited the spirit of a nation. Yet destiny had other plans for him. He was to forge his path in the crucible of revolution, amidst the fire and brimstone of artillery and the clarion calls for liberty. This man was Napoleon Bonaparte, and the siege of Toulon was his introduction to the stage of history.

But let us not rush ahead. The story of Napoleon's role in the French Revolution begins not on the fiery fields of Toulon but within the cobbled streets of Paris.

The Revolution arrived at Napoleon's doorstep while he was still in Paris, a student at the École Militaire. As the fortress of the Bastille fell to the revolutionaries in 1789, a symbolic victory against the oppressive old regime, Napoleon was there, a silent witness to the sweeping tide of history. He wrote to his brother, Joseph, that he believed the Revolution would cleanse France of her ailments and would save the state.

Yet, the Revolution was not merely an intellectual curiosity for Napoleon. The very fabric of French society was being torn asunder, and the winds of change were sweeping across the country. The nobility, the once untouchable elite, was now the target of popular ire, their privileges stripped away by the revolutionary National Assembly. As a member of the minor Corsican nobility studying at a military school traditionally reserved for the French elite, Napoleon found himself at the crossroads of these seismic societal shifts.

By 1793, the French Revolution had entered its most radical phase, marked by the rise of the Jacobins, the execution of Louis XVI, and the Reign of Terror under Maximilien Robespierre. It was a time of extremes, of lofty ideals and terrifying violence, and it was against this tumultuous backdrop that Napoleon was thrust into the stage of history.

Toulon, a strategic port city in the south of France, had rebelled against the revolutionary government and opened its gates to the British fleet. The Republican forces laid siege to the city, hoping to reclaim it for the Revolution. This was the crucible in which Napoleon's revolutionary journey was to be forged.

He was appointed as the artillery commander at Toulon due to a fortunate confluence of events. The Revolution, with its purges and paranoia, had left the French army bereft of experienced officers. Napoleon's superiors recognized his talents and, more importantly, his loyalty to the revolutionary cause. His appointment was a testament to the extraordinary opportunities provided by the Revolution for talented, ambitious young men.

The Siege of Toulon was a trial by fire for the young Bonaparte. His artillery skills, honed in the military academies, were to be tested in the crucible of war. The city was well fortified, and the presence of the British fleet added a formidable challenge. Yet, Napoleon was undaunted. He devised a strategy to isolate the city from the harbor, neutralizing the British naval advantage. It was a plan born of daring and innovation, traits that would come to define his military genius.

Napoleon's plan worked. After three months of intense fighting, the Republican forces, aided by Napoleon's artillery, took the city. His triumph did not go unnoticed. In the aftermath of the Siege, Napoleon was promoted to the rank of Brigadier General at the age of twenty-four. His successful strategy at Toulon marked him as a military mind of the first order and propelled him into the limelight. Toulon was the anvil upon which Bonaparte's reputation as a soldier was forged.

However, Napoleon's role in the Revolution was not limited to the battlefield. Back in Paris, he witnessed the ebb and flow of revolutionary fervor. He saw the fall of the monarchy, the rise of the radical Jacobins, and the terror they unleashed in their quest for purity. Napoleon was both a beneficiary and a critic of the Revolution. He admired its ideals of liberty, equality, and fraternity, yet abhorred its excesses and chaos.

His political acumen came to the fore in the aftermath of the Reign of Terror. The Jacobins had fallen, and the political landscape was in flux. In this period of uncertainty, Napoleon cast his lot with the new political power, the moderate Directory. His loyalty to the Directory was rewarded when he was appointed to command the French army in Italy, setting the stage for the next chapter of his life.

Napoleon's involvement in the French Revolution was a crucible that molded his character, honed his military skills, and set him on the path to power. It was during this time that he emerged from the obscurity of his Corsican roots to become a figure of national importance. The Revolution had, in a sense, created Napoleon.

Chapter 4:

Rise to Prominence

The prodigious flame that would eventually consume much of Europe had been kindled. With the soil of Toulon still clinging to his boots, Napoleon Bonaparte, the Corsican outsider, was beginning to insinuate himself into the heart of the Revolution, with the French Republic unwittingly playing host to the rise of its own potential overthrower.

At Toulon, he had earned his first taste of acclaim, demonstrating the kind of strategic brilliance and ruthless ambition that would become his signature. And yet, for the moment, his ambitions were still in check, restrained by the realities of his position within the intricate tapestry of French revolutionary politics.

In Paris, he worked diligently, navigating the treacherous political landscape with the same tactical skill he displayed on the battlefield. In 1795, Paris was more than just a city; it was an idea, an ever-shifting panorama of tumultuous politics and social upheaval. Here, the walls of the salons buzzed with heated debates and grand visions of France's future. Here, the tides of the Revolution were guided, and in those currents, Bonaparte began to see the threads of his own destiny.

These were precarious times, indeed. The young Republic was in a constant state of flux, its political life characterized by the ephemeral nature of power and the very real threat of the guillotine. France was a nation on the edge, and in this frenetic world, the young Corsican sought a niche, an opening that might allow him to advance.

His opportunity came, fittingly enough, amidst the chaos of revolt. The Thermidorian Reaction was in full swing, bringing with it a tumultuous period of insurrection and counter-revolution. In October 1795, the so-called "Day of 13 Vendémiaire", a royalist uprising erupted in the streets of Paris, a direct challenge to the young Republic. As fate would have it, the defense of the National Convention fell to Napoleon, who was then serving as the second commander of the Army of the Interior.

The young Corsican directed the artillery with the same skill and ruthless efficiency he had shown at Toulon, his 'whiff of grapeshot' decimating the royalist forces and safeguarding the fragile Republic. In the aftermath, he was hailed as the 'Savior of the French Republic'. Here, we see the first potent mix of Napoleon's military prowess and political expediency.

In the wake of his successful defense of the Convention, Napoleon was catapulted to national prominence. The Directorate, wary of his ambitions yet recognizing his value, appointed him to command the French army in Italy. It was an inspired choice, providing Napoleon with a theater in which to demonstrate his burgeoning military genius, whilst also conveniently relocating him far from the politically charged atmosphere of Paris.

In Italy, Napoleon found a canvas broad and grand enough to match his ambitions. The Italian campaign, often overlooked in the larger tableau of the Napoleonic Wars, would prove pivotal, both in Napoleon's personal narrative and the wider trajectory of Europe. Here was a stage where the prodigious Corsican could showcase his innovative military strategies and his exceptional command of both men and moment.

At the tender age of 26, he was already exhibiting a striking ability to marry audacity with calculation. He showed a keen understanding of the psychological component of warfare, his proclamations to his troops brimming with an infectious enthusiasm and unshakeable confidence. One such proclamation on the eve of battle demonstrates his remarkable charisma: "Soldiers! You are naked and ill fed! The Government owes you much and can give you nothing.... I will lead you into the most fertile plains in the world. Rich provinces, great cities will be in your power. There you will find honor, glory, and riches."

As he swept through Italy, his victories resonated beyond the battlefield. With each triumph, his political stock rose, and the collective consciousness of France began to take notice. The glory of his Italian campaign was inextricably linked to the glory of the Revolution. He was not only a military hero but a symbol of the Republic's vitality and resilience.

The young Corsican was rapidly becoming a household name, his exploits recounted in Parisian salons and rural taverns alike. His victories in Italy did more than just secure French dominance; they fed into the romantic myth of Napoleon, the tireless defender of the Republic, the brilliant tactician, the charismatic leader of men.

With this newfound fame came greater political leverage. As he carved his path through Italy, he showed a deft hand at diplomacy, negotiating the Treaty of Campo Formio with the Austrians. The treaty, which confirmed French control over most of Northern Italy and recognized the Rhine as France's eastern border, was hailed in Paris as a great triumph. The accolades for the treaty, much like the victories that preceded it, went to Napoleon. In the eyes of France, the Italian campaign was his triumph, a testament to his military and diplomatic genius.

With these feats, Napoleon Bonaparte was more than just a general; he was becoming an icon. A bright, blazing comet streaking across the turbulent sky of Revolutionary France. Unbeknownst to the Directory, they had cultivated the rise of a figure who would come to eclipse them, the Revolution, and indeed, the very idea of the Republic itself.

Yet, Napoleon was not the gravedigger of the Revolution, but its child. The irony is almost exquisite; the Revolution had, in its struggle to break free from the yoke of tyranny, birthed its own potential despot. But in these earlier days of his ascent, such a prophecy would have seemed absurd, the mere musing of the fearful or fantastical. At this point, the future Emperor was still the Republic's brightest star, a symbol of its ideals made manifest.

In the portrait of this period, we see a Napoleon fueled by ambition, a man possessed of a rare combination of talent, ruthlessness, and luck, who seized the opportunities offered by the turbulent times. It was these qualities that propelled him into the upper echelons of power, setting the stage for the next act of his extraordinary life.

As we delve deeper into the labyrinth of Napoleon's rise, we are reminded of the words of Edward Gibbon: "History is indeed little more than the register of the crimes, follies, and misfortunes of mankind." Yet, one might also argue that history is the tale of ambition, of determination and genius seizing the moment. Napoleon's rise from the tumultuous currents of the Revolution to the heights of power is testament to this. A Corsican by birth, French by circumstance, he was fast becoming a figure who would leave an indelible imprint on the pages of history.

Chapter 5

The Italian Campaign

When our gaze lands on the epoch of 1796, we are met with a breathtaking tapestry woven with the threads of conflict and conquest. At the center of this grand canvas, the verdant land of Italy lay, resplendent in its cultural heritage and turbulent in its dance with power. It was here that Napoleon Bonaparte, the Corsican revolutionary, would metamorphose into Napoleon, the conqueror.

In a momentous turn of events, Napoleon was appointed to the helm of the French 'Army of Italy'. He was an outsider, fresh-faced and, to many eyes, unproven in the arena of large-scale command. Yet, as the Corsican would soon prove, underestimating his tactical genius would be a grave error.

The condition of the French forces in Italy was dire. Napoleon found himself at the helm of a dispirited and ill-equipped army. Yet, displaying the tenacity and charisma that would become his hallmark, he rallied his troops with an impassioned address, promising them the bounty of Italy's fertile lands. His words breathed a new spirit into the beleaguered men, inspiring them to rise above their hardships.

The theater of conflict was no less challenging. Napoleon faced two formidable foes: the Austrian Habsburgs and their allies, the Piedmontese forces of the Kingdom of Sardinia. The combined strength of his adversaries hovered around 52,000 men, far outnumbering his own ragtag army of 37,000.

But numbers would prove insufficient to counter the tempest that was about to be unleashed. Napoleon implemented the strategy of central position, dividing his enemy's forces and defeating them in detail. He first targeted the Sardinians, defeating them at Montenotte and Millesimo, and then again at Mondovi. These victories led to the signing of the armistice at Cherasco, removing the Sardinians from the equation.

The Austrian forces were his next focus. At the Battle of Lodi, Napoleon led his army against the retreating Austrian forces, who numbered around 10,000 strong. It was a hard-fought engagement. The French charged across a narrow bridge under a hailstorm of Austrian fire, a bold move that resulted in a stunning victory. This victory left Lombardy in French control and marked a turning point in Napoleon's life. It was after this battle that he began to believe in his destiny, in his potential for greatness.

The Italian Campaign, however, was not merely a series of dazzling military victories. Napoleon proved himself to be an adept diplomat, courting the Italian nobility and the common populace alike. As towns fell to the French forces, he styled himself as a liberator, freeing the Italians from the clutches of Austrian oppression. He also cleverly played upon Italian nationalism, fostering resentment against foreign rule.

Beyond this, he started implementing French-style administrations, effectively transforming Italian states into sister republics under French influence. His capacity to intertwine military victories with political acumen, creating alliances that fortified his position, was truly remarkable.

Back in France, news of the Italian Campaign was met with mixed feelings. The common French citizen was captivated by the tales of this audacious general, who, against all odds, was delivering victory after victory. But among the political elite, Napoleon's escalating fame and overt ambition stirred unease, a whisper of apprehension about the power he was amassing.

For Napoleon, though, the Italian Campaign had set his stars on a seemingly unstoppable ascendancy. He was the national hero, celebrated in songs and toasted in Parisian salons. His image was proliferating across France, sowing the seeds of the Napoleon legend.

The Italian Campaign, then, was not a mere stepping stone to power. It was the crucible in which Napoleon was forged. It was here that the world witnessed the emergence of a leader who combined audacious battlefield tactics, strategic brilliance, and political cunning. It was in Italy that Napoleon

Bonaparte, the man, was transformed into Napoleon, the legend.

The Italian soil bore witness to Napoleon's might, his charisma, his relentless ambition. And, as we delve further into his life and reign, we shall observe how these traits would reappear, again and again, shaping not just his destiny but the course of history itself. But for now, let us linger a while longer on the sun-drenched plains of Italy, where a commander became a conqueror, and the Corsican Napoleon, an ordinary man, was transformed into NAPOLEON, the legend.

Chapter 6:

The Egyptian Expedition

As the dust settled on the Italian Campaign and Napoleon Bonaparte basked in the glow of his victories, he set his sights on a new horizon, a land of antiquity, shrouded in mystery - Egypt. With its golden sands and ancient pyramids, Egypt was a tantalizing prospect. A chapter of his story etched with the grandeur of pharaohs and the allure of an Oriental dream. Yet, beneath the shimmering facade, the Egyptian Expedition was a chess move of strategic mastery and a testament to Napoleon's boundless ambition.

The Egyptian Expedition was not born in a vacuum. It was a seed sown by a combination of geopolitical strategizing and Napoleon's personal ambitions. The primary objective was to disrupt Britain's trade routes to India, the jewel in its imperial crown. The Directory, governing France at the time, also saw the expedition as a way to export the ideals of the Revolution, albeit in the garb of colonial expansion. And, for Napoleon, it presented an opportunity to carve his name in the annals of history.

In May 1798, the French armada, a fleet of approximately 400 ships, sailed from Toulon. They carried with them an army of about 35,000 soldiers, not just men of war, but scholars, engineers, artists, and scientists, reflective of Napoleon's vision of not just military conquest but also intellectual and cultural expansion.

Upon their arrival, the French forces wasted no time. They stormed Alexandria, then headed for Cairo, the beating heart of Egypt. The Mamluk rulers, the de facto powers in Egypt, were unprepared for the French onslaught. The Battle of the Pyramids, fought on July 21, 1798, was a tactical masterstroke by Napoleon. Despite being outnumbered by the Mamluk forces of approximately 50,000 men, the French, disciplined and drilled, formed into their infamous infantry squares, a formation impervious to the Mamluk cavalry charges. The French emerged victorious, and Cairo fell into their hands. But victory on the battlefield was only part of the struggle.

Indeed, the occupation of Egypt was fraught with complexities. The cultural chasm between the French and the Egyptians was vast. Napoleon's initial attempts to position himself as a liberator and an ally to Islam had limited success. The administration he set up in Cairo was French at its core, an alien construct in a land deeply rooted in Islamic traditions. The resulting resentment among the local populace was palpable and would erupt in rebellions.

The military challenges, too, were mounting. The destruction of the French fleet by the British forces at the Battle of the Nile left the French forces stranded, an army without a fleet. The British, under Admiral Nelson, had dealt a devastating blow, seizing control of the Mediterranean and cutting off Napoleon's forces from France.

Further, the Ottoman Empire, who still held nominal control over Egypt, declared war on France, adding another enemy to the growing list. A successful campaign against an Ottoman army at the Battle of Mount Tabor in 1799 was a fleeting moment of respite in what was fast becoming a quagmire.

Napoleon's Egyptian Expedition was more than a military campaign. It was also a vast intellectual enterprise. The scholars accompanying the army embarked on an ambitious project of studying and documenting Egypt's history, culture, flora, fauna, and more. The resultant work, the 'Description de l'Égypte,' was a monumental achievement, pioneering Egyptology and leaving an indelible mark on the European imagination.

Yet, for all its cultural and scientific achievements, the Egyptian Expedition was a strategic misstep. The attrition of war, the unforgiving climate, and diseases had whittled down the French forces. The loss of their fleet, the growing hostility of the local populace, and the arrival of an Anglo-Ottoman force spelled the end for the French in Egypt.

In August 1799, Napoleon, in a move that would spark controversy, slipped away from Egypt, leaving his army in the hands of General Jean Baptiste Kléber. The man who had entered Egypt as a conqueror left as a fugitive, escaping on a small frigate and slipping through the British blockade. His reputation at home remained largely untarnished, his failures in Egypt overshadowed by his Italian victories. Yet, his departure left an army abandoned and a land in chaos.

The Egyptian Expedition was a chapter in Napoleon's life riddled with paradoxes. It was a military adventure laced with cultural exploration, an ambitious gambit that ended in strategic failure, and a journey that elevated Napoleon's stature while laying bare his limitations.

In the final reckoning, the sands of Egypt proved treacherous for Napoleon Bonaparte. His dreams of Eastern glory were buried deep in its shifting dunes. And yet, even in failure, the expedition held a mirror to the complexities and contradictions that marked the man and his mission, the dreamer and the doer, the scholar, and the soldier. It was a testament to his audacity, his unyielding ambition, and his ability to dare where others faltered. Despite its ultimate failure, the Egyptian Expedition remains a fascinating chapter in the narrative of Napoleon Bonaparte. For it was here, amidst the timeless sands of Egypt, that the world caught a glimpse of the man behind the legend, the mortal behind the myth.

Chapter 7:

The Coup of 18 Brumaire

Amidst the shifting sands of Egyptian deserts and against the backdrop of towering pyramids, Napoleon had envisioned an empire of his own making. His ambitions, however, were not confined to the banks of the Nile. Back on French soil, a different sort of pyramid was being constructed; a political pyramid, a power structure where the vertex was yet to be occupied. As he navigated his Egyptian odyssey, Napoleon's gaze was firmly set on this vertex. The fulcrum that would tilt this in his favor came to be known as the Coup of 18 Brumaire.

In France, the dawn of November 9, 1799, or 18 Brumaire Year VIII, according to the revolutionary calendar, broke with the promise of another day in the throes of the French Revolution. The political architecture, shaped by the relentless chisel of revolutionary fervor, was trembling under its own weight. The Directory, the five-man committee presiding over the French Republic, was caught in the vortex of economic instability, military crises, and public dissatisfaction. A change was imminent, a new balance of power was on the horizon. The question was not if, but when, and more importantly, in whose favor.

The orchestrator of this upheaval was not to be found among the incumbent Directors but among the military ranks. Napoleon Bonaparte, the victorious general of the Italian Campaign and the conqueror of Egypt, had returned to France. His military triumphs and the charisma that followed them were the perfect foil to the Directory's disarray.

The idea of a coup had not been Napoleon's brainchild. It was a plan conceived by Emmanuel Joseph Sieyès, one of the Directors, who had grown disillusioned with the ineptitude of the Directory. He envisioned a stronger government, one fortified with the tenets of the Constitution but guided by a robust executive authority. Sieyès saw in Napoleon the instrument to realize this vision.

Napoleon, for his part, recognized the opportunity the situation presented. The Directory, weakened and discredited, was ripe for overthrowing. The public, fatigued by the constant turmoil, yearned for stability. The military, the power that could tip the scales, was loyal to him. The stage was set.

The coup unfolded over three days. The first act began on 18 Brumaire with Napoleon's appointment as the commander of the Home Army, effectively putting the military might of Paris under his control. However, the real drama unfolded on the following day, 19 Brumaire, in the

Council of Five Hundred, the lower house of the French legislature.

Napoleon, flanked by armed grenadiers, stormed into the council, appealing for their support. But the move backfired. The legislators, rather than being swayed, erupted in outrage, accusing him of violating the sanctity of the Council. The scene was chaotic, the situation teetering on the edge of disaster.

Napoleon's brother, Lucien, then president of the Council, played a crucial role at this juncture. He managed to rally the soldiers outside the Council, painting a dramatic picture of his brother's life being in danger. The soldiers, loyal to Napoleon, stormed into the Council, dispersing the deputies. Thus, ended the second act of the coup, not with a smooth transition of power, but with a scene of pandemonium.

The coup concluded on 20 Brumaire, with the legislative councils, coerced and stripped of their dissenting elements, appointing a provisional government, the Consulate. This new power structure was composed of three Consuls, but make no mistake, the First Consul, Napoleon Bonaparte, held the reins.

The Coup of 18 Brumaire marked a critical crossroads in the French Revolution and Napoleon's life. It was the end of the French Republic born out of the Revolution and the beginning of a new phase where power was consolidated under Napoleon.

The coup was more than just a power grab; it was a testament to Napoleon's political acumen. He had entered the political arena not as a player but as a pawn in Sieyès's game. But as the events unfolded, Napoleon deftly turned the tables. Sieyès, the architect of the coup, became a peripheral figure, while Napoleon, the instrument, seized the center stage.

In the grand tapestry of the French Revolution, the Coup of 18 Brumaire is a pivotal thread. It marked the moment when the Revolution, which had begun as a crusade against monarchy and absolute power, ended up bestowing absolute power on a single individual. The irony was hard to miss.

However, the coup was not just about the seizure of power; it was about what was done with that power. It laid the foundation for a series of reforms that would shape France and leave a lasting imprint on the world.

The Coup of 18 Brumaire was the precipice from which Napoleon Bonaparte leaped, not into the abyss of uncertainty, but onto the firm ground of control. The French Republic had provided the prologue to this leap, and the French Empire, with Napoleon at its helm, was about to script the main act. The coup marked the end of one tumultuous chapter and the beginning of another, equally, if not more, momentous one. But that is a tale for another time.

For now, let us take a moment to reflect upon the coup and its significance, not just for Napoleon, but for France and indeed the world. For it was in this moment, this brazen seizure of power, that the seeds of the Napoleonic era were sown.

Chapter 8:

Reforms and Innovations

The Coup of 18 Brumaire had dramatically altered the political landscape of France. The Directory was dissolved and the Consulate took its place, with Napoleon Bonaparte as the First Consul. But this change in governance was not an end in itself; it was the gateway to a larger and more profound transformation that would reshape France at its very core. The architect of this transformation was, unsurprisingly, Napoleon.

His first significant step was the establishment of the "Constitution of the Year VIII." This constitution, accepted in a popular vote, affirmed the establishment of the Consulate and officially designated Napoleon as the First Consul, vested with broad executive powers. Despite being an outcome of a coup, this constitution symbolized the aspirations of stability, order, and effective governance that were so keenly desired by the weary French public. However, the constitution was not merely a charter of government; it was the canvas on which Napoleon began to sketch his vision of a new France.

Napoleon's primary focus was to restore stability and order to the chaos-ridden French society. But his approach was not limited to rigid enforcement of law and order. He realized that societal stability could only be achieved when there is economic stability. To this end, he set about rebuilding France's economy.

The impact of the Revolution and the subsequent political turmoil had left the French economy in ruins. Inflation was rampant, and the national debt was astronomical. The financial situation of the state was precarious at best. The first step to economic rejuvenation was the regularization of state finances. To achieve this, Napoleon instituted the Bank of France in 1800. This institution, responsible for issuing a stable currency and providing loans to the government, was instrumental in stabilizing the French economy and laying the foundation for economic growth.

Concurrent to these financial reforms, Napoleon also took steps to revitalize French industry and trade. He fostered industry through government patronage and protective tariffs. As for trade, the internal barriers that had long hindered the free movement of goods within France were dismantled. These reforms not only propelled economic growth but also engendered a new class of wealthy industrialists and traders, adding a fresh dynamism to the French economy.

While economic reforms were essential, Napoleon was aware that they alone were not enough to forge a new society.

A stable society, he understood, needed a solid educational system. The French education system, fragmented and uneven, was inadequate for this task. To address this, Napoleon introduced a series of educational reforms.

At the heart of Napoleon's education reforms was the establishment of the University of France in 1808, an overarching body that controlled all levels of education. Under this system, state-run schools, known as lycées, were established, which provided a standardized curriculum throughout the country. This system not only democratized education but also served to instill civic values and a sense of national identity among the students. Napoleon, ever the military man, also established special military schools to cultivate the future officers of his army.

These education reforms were instrumental in the creation of an educated citizenry that was not only equipped with the necessary skills but also imbued with a sense of loyalty to the state. Napoleon was shrewd enough to understand that an educated populace was not just an asset but also a bulwark against instability.

While the economic and educational reforms were crucial components of Napoleon's transformational agenda, the most lasting and impactful of his reforms was the establishment of a new legal code, famously known as the Napoleonic Code. This monumental work, a unifying legal code, was an audacious attempt to instill order and rationality into the disparate and often conflicting legal systems that were in force in different parts of France.

The Napoleonic Code was an embodiment of many Enlightenment ideals. It established the principles of equality before the law, safeguarded civil liberties, and affirmed the rights to property. However, it was not a perfect document. The Code was silent on many aspects of individual rights, particularly those pertaining to women, and did not challenge the social hierarchies that had started to re-emerge in France.

Despite its shortcomings, the Napoleonic Code was revolutionary in its implications. By establishing a uniform set of laws, it eliminated the legal confusion that had long plagued France. More importantly, it embedded the revolutionary ideals of equality and individual rights into the very fabric of French society.

The reforms and innovations introduced by Napoleon during his tenure as the First Consul were transformative in the truest sense of the word. They helped stabilize a society in turmoil, revitalized a beleaguered economy, created an educated citizenry, and laid the groundwork for a legal system that continues to influence civil law around the world.

Napoleon, the brilliant general, had shown that he could be an equally adept statesman. His reforms were not just about restructuring the society; they were about reimagining it. Under his rule, France was not merely recovering from the upheavals of the Revolution; it was evolving into something entirely new. As he was consolidating his hold on power, Napoleon was also reshaping France. He was laying the foundation of a state that, despite its future tribulations, would emerge stronger, more unified, and more resilient.

Chapter 9:

Road to the Throne

Napoleon had ascended to the position of First Consul of France in the aftermath of the coup of 18 Brumaire, but the man who had emerged from the chaotic politics of post-Revolutionary France was not one to be content with this position of power alone. Power, after all, was a ladder, and there were still more rungs to climb. Napoleon Bonaparte, ever the strategist, was already eyeing the throne.

But the path to monarchy in a country that had so recently decapitated its king in a wave of republican fervor was a treacherous one. It would take all of Napoleon's formidable cunning, political acumen, and talent for manipulation to pave the road to the throne.

The foundation for this grand ambition was laid in the Constitution of the Year VIII. While establishing the Consulate, this constitution had made Napoleon the First Consul, but more importantly, it had made him First Consul for a ten-year term. A decade, Napoleon knew, was enough time to engineer the circumstances that would propel him to greater heights.

In the early years of the Consulate, Napoleon had demonstrated his administrative and legislative prowess, breathing life back into a nation ravaged by years of revolution and internal strife. His reforms had stabilized the economy, restructured education, and created a unified legal system. France, under Napoleon's leadership, had begun to find its feet again.

The restoration of order and prosperity was not simply a matter of necessity for Napoleon; it was also a strategy. He understood that the French people, fatigued by years of chaos, yearned for stability. He also knew that a populace enjoying the fruits of economic prosperity and societal order would be more amenable to further changes in the political structure of the nation.

Alongside his administrative efforts, Napoleon worked on crafting an image of himself that would endear him to the public. He was frequently depicted in paintings and newspaper accounts as a decisive leader, a protector of the people, and a symbol of stability and order. He was portrayed not as a dictator, but as a benevolent leader guiding France out of turbulent times.

This careful public relations campaign was complemented by Napoleon's deft manipulation of France's political institutions. He centralized power, co-opting or sidelining those who opposed him. By rendering the legislative body toothless, Napoleon effectively made the Consulate an autocracy.

As Napoleon's power within the state grew, so too did his popularity among the people. His victories in the military arena were celebrated with fervor, and his administrative successes were applauded. Napoleon had skillfully turned public opinion in his favor.

The final piece of the puzzle fell into place when a royalist plot to assassinate Napoleon was foiled in 1804. The event, known as the Plot of the Rue Saint-Nicaise, provided Napoleon with the perfect excuse to push his agenda forward. In the aftermath of the failed assassination attempt, he argued that the instability of the Consulate was inviting such threats. France, he posited, needed the continuity and stability that only a hereditary monarchy could provide.

This argument struck a chord with a populace tired of the constant turmoil and threats to their hard-won stability. With public opinion behind him and political institutions firmly under his control, Napoleon made his move. He put forth a proposal to establish a hereditary empire, with himself as Emperor. The proposal was put to a national vote in a plebiscite, and it passed overwhelmingly.

The plebiscite was undoubtedly manipulated, with opposition suppressed and votes inflated, but the outcome reflected a reality: the French people were willing to accept a monarchy if it promised to deliver continued stability and prosperity. The ghost of the guillotine, it seemed, was not enough to deter them from this path.

The road to the throne, treacherous as it was, had been traversed successfully. Napoleon Bonaparte, the Corsican outsider who had risen to prominence in the fires of the Revolution, had achieved the unthinkable. He had turned a republic born out of a vehement rejection of monarchy into an empire, with himself at its helm.

But Napoleon's ambition was not sated with mere power. He was keenly aware that to truly secure his position, he needed to drape his rule in the cloak of legitimacy. And in the Europe of the time, legitimacy came from one source: the Church. The man who had tamed the Revolution, manipulated public opinion, and outmaneuvered his political opponents was about to stage his most audacious spectacle yet: his own coronation.

Chapter 10:

Coronation as Emperor

In the grand tapestry of Napoleon Bonaparte's life, there is perhaps no scene quite as opulent, as audacious, as the coronation ceremony that declared him the Emperor of the French. It was an event that proclaimed to France, and the wider world, that the age of revolution was over and the era of Napoleon had begun.

The date was December 2, 1804, a chilly winter's day, when Napoleon Bonaparte ascended the steps of Notre Dame Cathedral in Paris. The location was significant; it was not only the religious heart of France but also a venue steeped in royal history. Choosing Notre Dame was a deliberate move, aligning Napoleon with the glorious heritage of France's past kings, and announcing a fresh chapter in the nation's destiny.

The coronation, though steeped in symbolism, was also a spectacle of immense extravagance. Amid the stone cold solemnity of Notre Dame, a massive coronation theatre had been constructed to accommodate a crowd of 4000 nobles, dignitaries, and members of government. The stage was set, and Paris held its breath.

On the day of the ceremony, Napoleon and his wife, Josephine, arrived in a lavish procession that wound its way through the streets of Paris, drawing thousands of spectators. It was a masterstroke of public relations, emphasizing the pomp and grandeur of the occasion, and instilling in the public consciousness an image of Napoleon not as a military general or a political leader, but as a monarch.

The ceremony itself was meticulously choreographed, a dramatic blend of traditional ritual and innovative symbolism. Amid the familiar trappings of royal investiture—the crimson velvet robes, the ceremonial swords, the gleaming scepter—there were details that pointedly set Napoleon's coronation apart from those of the Bourbon kings.

One of these was the crown itself. Rather than the traditional Capetian crown, Napoleon opted for a new, specially designed laurel-leaf crown of gold. This decision was deeply symbolic; it not only signified a break from the past, but also aligned Napoleon with the Roman emperors, further strengthening his claim to absolute power.

Yet the moment that resonates most vividly from that day, the gesture that shook the foundations of tradition and sent a clear message to the world, was the act of crowning itself. Instead of allowing Pope Pius VII, who had been invited to preside over the ceremony, to place the crown on his head, Napoleon took the crown from the Pope's hands and placed it on his own head.

In this moment, Napoleon was not merely defying centuries of tradition; he was making a profound political statement. By crowning himself, he was asserting his authority as derived not from divine right, not from the Church, and not from the will of the nobility, but from his own accomplishments and the will of the people. He was, in effect, the self-made Emperor.

Following Napoleon's self-crowning, he proceeded to crown Josephine as Empress, further cementing his imperial status and strengthening the dynastic implications of the event. It was an act of pomp and spectacle, but it was also a touching personal moment between husband and wife, humanizing them amidst the grandeur of the occasion.

But Napoleon's coronation was not merely a celebration of his ascent to the throne; it was also a platform to demonstrate the direction of his imperial rule. The presence of the constitutional bodies at the ceremony signified that Napoleon intended to rule within the framework of the Constitution, albeit a Constitution heavily manipulated to favor his autocratic rule. It was a delicate balancing act, assuring the French people that their Emperor was not a tyrant, but a guardian of the Republic's principles.

The ceremony concluded with a grand Te Deum, a traditional hymn of praise and thanksgiving, filling the hallowed halls of Notre Dame with soaring music. As Napoleon and Josephine exited the cathedral, they were met with a twenty-one gun salute, a final, resounding declaration of the birth of a new era.

The coronation of Napoleon Bonaparte was more than a ceremony; it was a calculated performance designed to legitimize his rule and solidify his position in the eyes of the French public and the wider world. With the precision of a military strategist and the flair of a showman, Napoleon had used the coronation to craft an indelible image of himself as a leader: powerful, legitimate, and unlike any other.

In the aftermath of the ceremony, the streets of Paris erupted into celebration. Fireworks lit up the winter sky, and the air was filled with the sound of cheering crowds and pealing bells. Whether out of genuine joy or careful politeness, the city appeared to embrace their new Emperor.

The coronation had achieved what Napoleon had intended: it was not only an endorsement of his ascension to the throne, but it was also a tacit acceptance of the new political order he had established. Napoleon had staked his claim to the throne of France, and for better or worse, the nation had acquiesced. The road to power had reached its end; Napoleon Bonaparte, the son of Corsican nobles, was now Emperor of the French.

Chapter 11:

Napoleon and Josephine

In the annals of French history, few love stories have stirred as much fascination as that of Napoleon Bonaparte and Josephine de Beauharnais. Their relationship, fervent and multifaceted, navigated the rugged terrains of political turmoil, personal tribulation, and the relentless pursuit of power.

Josephine, christened Marie Josèphe Rose Tascher de la Pagerie, was a creole beauty from the verdant island of Martinique. She had known hardship; widowhood, the destitution of the French Revolution, and the cruel guillotine which claimed her first husband, Alexandre de Beauharnais. Yet, she was a woman of remarkable resilience, whose charm and sophistication held Parisian society in thrall.

Napoleon, a fiery Corsican, was still just a promising military officer when their paths crossed in the late 18th century. His initial attraction to Josephine was almost visceral, an admixture of infatuation, respect, and an undeniable affinity for her grace and worldliness.

Their union, formalized in a civil ceremony on March 9, 1796, was not a customary alliance of convenience. Their fervent correspondence during periods of separation attests to a genuine affection, a magnetic pull that went beyond societal expectations. It was as though they recognized in each other a kindred spirit, a fellow navigator on the stormy seas of a changing France.

But as the saying goes, 'the course of true love never did run smooth'. Theirs was a union tested by the cruel exigencies of time, duty, and the insatiable hunger for power. One such challenge was the specter of infidelity that cast a shadow over their relationship.

Rumors of Josephine's extramarital affair during Napoleon's Italian campaign sparked tumultuous waves of jealousy and suspicion. The whispers of her liaison with Lieutenant Hippolyte Charles stirred Napoleon's ire, yet, he remained firmly entranced by his "Josephine", a testament to the depth of his affection. It is a poignant reminder that even a man destined to become Emperor was not immune to the vulnerabilities of the human heart.

Despite this, and perhaps because of it, Josephine's influence on Napoleon was transformative. Her understanding of social dynamics, her charm and diplomatic finesse, provided him with a crucially different perspective. She offered him a bridge to the French elite, a way to temper his military bluntness with the refined nuance of high society.

As the consort of Napoleon, Josephine was far from a mere ornament. She brought her own strengths to the fore, using her social acumen to serve as a de facto diplomat at the Tuileries Palace. Her soirees were a shimmering tableau of the French elite, her gracious presence serving as an antidote to the rigid severity of Napoleon's rule.

But as the years waned on, a stark reality loomed over them. The absence of a male heir from their union gnawed at Napoleon, becoming a throbbing ache as his reign over France solidified. Their intense love story, however, was destined for an end as Napoleon sought to secure his dynasty.

In December 1809, the painful divorce unfolded. Yet, the depth of their connection was such that even this painful rupture was underscored by enduring respect and affection. Napoleon's tears, and his assurance of Josephine's continued prominence, painted a picture of a love undimmed by circumstance.

Their separation did not spell an end to Josephine's role in Napoleon's life. He ensured her comfort and social standing, and often sought her advice on matters of personal and political importance. Their relationship had evolved, yet the bond remained.

Their love story, with its passionate beginnings, tumultuous middle, and poignant end, serves as a fascinating microcosm of the Napoleonic era. It was not merely a personal affair, but a powerful narrative interwoven with the fabric of a nation in flux.

Legend has it that even in his final moments on the desolate island of Saint Helena, Napoleon whispered Josephine's name. This enduring love resonates through the centuries, an enduring echo of a time, a man, and a woman who indelibly shaped the course of history.

In the dance of power and love that was Napoleon and Josephine's relationship, we see the personal dimensions of historical events. Their love, their trials, their inevitable separation – each forms a critical piece in the complex puzzle of understanding Napoleon Bonaparte, the man who once stood astride the world like a colossus.

Chapter 12:

Conquests and Coalitions

In the annals of warfare, few periods in history resonate with as much strategic brilliance, heart-rending tragedy, and grand spectacle as the Napoleonic Wars. The stage was set for a tumultuous upheaval of the existing world order. Napoleon, now standing astride the French Empire like a colossus, eyed the horizon with the gaze of a conqueror, his ambitions not limited to the bounds of his beloved France. This period saw the rise of the Napoleonic grand strategy, an innovative and relentless approach to warfare that would both enthrall and horrify the powers of Europe.

Napoleon's military genius was multifaceted, founded on a keen understanding of the strengths and weaknesses of his own forces and those of his adversaries. His army, often referred to as the Grande Armée, was a force to be reckoned with. It was an amalgamation of experienced veterans, ardent young soldiers, and skilled commanders, all driven by an unwavering belief in their leader. They were as diverse as the nation they represented, a melting pot of men from all walks of life united under the tricolor banner of Revolutionary France.

On the other side of the chessboard, a league of adversaries emerged. The War of the Second Coalition had already seen a group of European powers band together to curb Napoleon's ambitions. Yet, they had been humbled on the battlefields of Marengo and Hohenlinden. As Napoleon's influence expanded, so did the resolve of his enemies. Britain, Austria, Prussia, Russia, and a host of smaller states rallied under the banner of various coalitions, each alliance an attempt to balance the scales against the seemingly unstoppable force of Napoleon.

The Battle of Austerlitz, often referred to as the Battle of the Three Emperors, offers a vivid illustration of Napoleon's strategic acumen. Facing the combined forces of Russia and Austria in December 1805, Napoleon found himself outmatched in numbers. Yet, he turned this apparent disadvantage into a strategic ruse. By deliberately weakening his right flank, he lured the allies into a premature attack. Then, at the critical moment, he launched a ferocious counter-offensive that shattered the enemy center, resulting in a crushing victory for France.

At Jena-Auerstedt in 1806, Napoleon demonstrated another facet of his grand strategy: the use of rapid, concentrated movements to disrupt enemy communications and supply lines. Despite facing a numerically superior Prussian force, he divided his own forces and managed to defeat the enemy in detail, inflicting a defeat from which Prussia would take years to recover.

In battle after battle, from the snow-swept fields of Eylau to the sun-baked plains of Wagram, Napoleon employed his revolutionary corps system to great effect. Instead of a single unwieldy mass, his army was divided into self-sufficient corps, each capable of independent operation. This enabled rapid marches, surprise attacks, and the ability to converge on the battlefield from multiple directions, often confounding his enemies.

Yet, while these victories are often highlighted, one should not forget the toll of such relentless warfare. The Grande Armée, while formidable, was not an inexhaustible resource. Casualties mounted, veterans were replaced with raw recruits, and the logistical challenges of campaigning in foreign lands put a significant strain on French resources. Even the indomitable spirit of the French soldier had its limits, as the hardships of war began to take a toll on morale.

Despite the odds, Napoleon's strategic vision, combined with the grit and resilience of his soldiers, led to a series of stunning victories that reshaped the map of Europe. But these victories came at a cost. Each coalition that was defeated gave rise to another, as Europe united against the shared threat posed by Napoleon's ambitions.

The Napoleonic Wars were characterized by a complex interplay of strategy, bravery, and the harsh realities of warfare. Yet, they were also defined by the emergence of a new style of warfare, one that combined speed, flexibility, and a focus on decisive battles rather than drawn-out sieges. This period saw the rise of the 'nation in arms', a concept that would later influence both the scale and nature of warfare in the centuries to come.

In the grand tapestry of the Napoleonic era, the Conquests and Coalitions stand out as a testament to the indomitable will of a man and a nation. They serve as a powerful reminder of the dual nature of warfare - its potential to bring about change and its inevitable cost. Whether on the snow-covered fields of Russia, the sun-kissed plains of Spain, or the rolling hills of central Europe, the echo of these battles continues to reverberate through the annals of history, a stark reminder of a time when a single man's ambition shook the world.

Chapter 13

The Battle of Austerlitz

In the theater of war, few battles echo with the seismic significance of the Battle of Austerlitz. It remains not just a testament to Napoleon Bonaparte's military genius but also a touchstone for the dynamism that defined his reign. Austerlitz was more than just a battle; it was a symphony of tactics and audacity that would cast long shadows over Europe and etch the name of Napoleon into the annals of history.

The morning of December 2, 1805, bore the promise of a typical winter's day in Moravia. An eerie calmness blanketed the Pratzen Heights as the sun slowly pierced through the fog. It is said that when Napoleon saw the emerging sun, he exclaimed, "Behold the sun of Austerlitz!" Little did he know that this sun would not only burn through the fog but also illuminate one of his greatest military triumphs.

Napoleon's forces at Austerlitz were a study in diversity and resilience. Veterans of the Italian campaigns rubbed shoulders with eager conscripts, creating a vibrant tapestry of French society. The strength of the Grande Armée, nearly 68,000 strong, was not merely in its numbers or the crackle of musketry, but in the collective conviction of its soldiers.

Each man saw himself as a cog in the larger machinery of the Napoleonic war machine, all turning together under the confident gaze of their Emperor.

Facing Napoleon was the combined strength of the Austro-Russian armies, a formidable force of approximately 90,000 soldiers under the command of Tsar Alexander I and Emperor Francis II. The coalition forces were seasoned warriors, drilled to perfection, and buoyed by their numerical superiority. They bore the weight of their nations' hopes, standing as bulwarks against Napoleon's relentless march across Europe.

But Napoleon was not daunted by the odds. Instead, he turned them to his advantage with a masterstroke of tactical deception. He presented a deliberately weak right flank to the enemy, inviting an attack. The Austro-Russian forces, taking the bait, poured their energies into exploiting this perceived weakness. However, in their eagerness to seize the opportunity, they neglected their strategic position on the Pratzen Heights.

The heart of the battle lay in the controlled chaos of Napoleon's strategy. He had presented the enemy with a lure, a feigned vulnerability, and they had taken it. Now, with the enemy drawn away from the Heights and their lines stretched thin, Napoleon struck back with the full might of his reserves.

The French assault was as relentless as it was unexpected. Marshal Soult's IV Corps stormed the Heights with a fervor that was nothing short of astonishing. The coalition forces, caught off-guard and fragmented, were unable to mount a coordinated defense. The battle, though fierce and fraught with peril, began to swing decisively in favor of the French.

Napoleon, surveying the battlefield from the Heights, orchestrated his forces like a maestro, issuing orders and directing movements with an uncanny sense of timing. The final stroke came when he ordered his cavalry to crash into the exposed flanks of the enemy forces, wreaking havoc in their ranks and shattering their morale. The Austro-Russian forces, facing such a ferocious onslaught, began to crumble.

The victory at Austerlitz was not just a testament to Napoleon's strategic brilliance but also to the courage and determination of the French soldiers. They had faced an enemy superior in numbers and had not only held their ground but had turned the tide of battle.

However, the battle was also a chilling reminder of the brutal reality of war. The field of Austerlitz bore silent witness to the cost of victory, littered with the fallen from both sides. While the French reveled in their triumph, it was a joy tempered by the sight of comrades who had paid the ultimate price.

In the aftermath of Austerlitz, Napoleon was not just a victorious general; he was the master of Europe. He had faced a formidable coalition and had emerged victorious, cementing his reputation as one of history's greatest military tacticians. The Battle of Austerlitz had far-reaching implications, reshaping the geopolitical landscape of Europe and setting the stage for Napoleon's continued dominance.

Yet, for all its significance, Austerlitz also showcased the paradox of Napoleon. Here was a man who could display remarkable ingenuity and ruthless efficiency on the battlefield, and yet remained deeply human, touched by the sacrifices of his men. His victory at Austerlitz was not just a military triumph, but a manifestation of his complex persona: a man as capable of inspiring profound loyalty as he was of instilling deep-seated fear.

In the grand narrative of Napoleon Bonaparte's life, the Battle of Austerlitz stands as a pivotal chapter. It is a testament to his military genius, his indomitable spirit, and the devotion of his troops. As the sun of Austerlitz set, it cast long shadows of a future filled with both triumph and tragedy, a future that would continue to be shaped by the will and ambition of Napoleon.

Chapter 14:

The Continental System

In the annals of military history, battles are typically thought of as physical confrontations – armies meeting on the battlefield in a test of strength and strategy. Yet, under the expansive reign of Napoleon Bonaparte, warfare took on a new and elusive form, one not bound by traditional constraints. The theater of conflict was no longer confined to the battlefield but had extended to encompass the economic heartlands of nations.

This chapter traces the subtle machinations of the Continental System – Napoleon's masterstroke of economic warfare against Britain. It was a stratagem designed to strangle Britain's economic lifeline, to undermine the strength of the nation not through direct confrontation but by systematically isolating it from the rest of Europe.

In November 1806, from the opulent halls of Berlin's royal palace, Napoleon issued the Berlin Decree, the foundation stone of the Continental System. It was a stark proclamation, an absolute embargo on British trade with the nations under Napoleon's control or influence. The decree was more than just an economic sanction; it was a gauntlet thrown in the face of Britain, a nonviolent yet potent declaration of war.

Napoleon's strategy was a novel one. The common belief of the era was that war was won on the battlefield, with cannons, rifles, and the blood of brave men. Yet, Napoleon recognized that a nation's power was not only in its military might but in its economic vitality. Britain, though an island nation, was a commercial powerhouse, its economy fueled by trade with the European mainland. By denying Britain access to these markets, Napoleon aimed to cripple its economy and, by extension, its ability to wage war.

This economic siege was ambitious in its scope, encompassing not only the territories directly under Napoleon's control but also those of his allies and vassals. From the bustling ports of Amsterdam to the azure coasts of Naples, all were to close their gates to British goods. Even Russia, under Tsar Alexander I, was coerced into compliance, though this would later prove to be a double-edged sword.

In theory, the Continental System was a formidable strategy, a stranglehold that threatened to squeeze the life out of Britain's economy. Yet, in practice, it proved to be a complicated endeavor. Enforcing such an extensive blockade required not only resources but also the willingness of all parties involved. It soon became evident that the loyalty of Napoleon's allies was not as steadfast as he had hoped.

The inherent difficulties of enforcing the Continental System were amplified by Britain's robust response. The British government, recognizing the danger posed by Napoleon's embargo, enacted its own counter-blockade. The Orders in Council of 1807 declared all ports from which the British were excluded to be under a state of blockade, severely restricting neutral trade and turning the North Sea into a British lake.

This move triggered a cascade of unforeseen consequences. Countries that had previously remained neutral, most notably the United States, were pulled into the fray. American ships, caught between the British blockade and Napoleon's Continental System, became pawns in this invisible war. The resulting tensions would eventually culminate in the War of 1812, an indirect yet significant result of Napoleon's economic warfare.

The true impact of the Continental System, however, lies not in its foreign policy implications but in its effects on the common people. Across Europe, from the vineyards of France to the farmlands of Russia, ordinary citizens bore the brunt of the embargo. The absence of British goods led to skyrocketing prices and widespread discontent, fueling the flames of resistance against Napoleon's rule.

In France, the situation was particularly dire. The blockade had cut off supplies of raw materials, leading to a slowdown in industrial production and a surge in unemployment. The people, already weary from years of war, began to question the wisdom of their Emperor's policies.

Napoleon, in his pursuit of victory over Britain, had unintentionally waged war on his own people. His ambitious Continental System, though innovative, was not the decisive blow he had envisioned. Instead, it became a slow-burning fuse, eroding the foundations of his Empire from within.

Even so, the Continental System was not a complete failure. It did succeed in inflicting considerable damage on Britain's economy, leading to social unrest and political turmoil. Yet, Britain, buoyed by its naval dominance and the resilience of its people, weathered the storm.

Looking back, the Continental System serves as a stark reminder of the power and peril of economic warfare. It was a bold attempt to redefine the rules of engagement, a strategy as innovative as it was flawed. Yet, in the grand tapestry of Napoleon Bonaparte's life, it remains a significant thread, a testament to his unyielding ambition and his capacity for audacious gambits.

In the end, the Continental System is a poignant symbol of the Napoleonic era – a time of relentless upheaval and uncharted ventures. It speaks to the paradox of Napoleon – a man of vision who often failed to foresee the repercussions of his actions. A ruler whose strength lay not only in his command of the battlefield but also in his audacious attempts to control the intricate and elusive landscapes of global economics.

Chapter 15:

The Peninsular War

The annals of military history seldom find their origin in the confines of a royal palace. Yet, it was within such ornate walls, amidst the glittering chandeliers and velvety drapes, that the stage was set for the Peninsular War, a brutal conflict that would burn through the heart of Spain and Portugal and carve indelible scars into the legacy of Napoleon Bonaparte.

In 1807, the Palace of Fontainebleau in France was witness to a fateful pact, one that bore the signature of a once-mighty monarch. The Treaty of Fontainebleau, signed by Spain's King Charles IV, authorized the passage of French troops through Spanish territory to conquer Portugal, a recalcitrant ally of Britain. Little did the Spanish monarch know that this pact would be the catalyst for one of the bloodiest chapters in Iberian history, marking the start of six long years of turmoil and resistance.

But let us not rush ahead. The tableau unfolds methodically, the brushstrokes of history guided by the hand of time. French troops under General Junot entered Portugal in November 1807. The Portuguese army, numbering some 16,000 regulars and ill-prepared militia, was hardly a match for Junot's well-drilled force of 25,000. Despite attempts at resistance, the capital of Lisbon fell within a month, a grim harbinger of the events to come.

A mere whisper of Napoleon's ambitions was enough to kindle the flames of unease. As French armies swarmed the Iberian Peninsula, Spain found itself teetering on the precipice of revolt. The subsequent abdication of Charles IV in favor of his son, Ferdinand VII, merely served to stoke the embers, the Spanish populace growing increasingly wary of French encroachment.

By May 1808, the spark of rebellion had ignited into a conflagration. Uprisings broke out across Spain, the people rising in defiance against the French occupiers. This marked the beginning of the Peninsular War, a conflict characterized by a brutal fusion of conventional warfare and unremitting guerilla resistance. The French troops, who numbered approximately 280,000 at the peak of the conflict, found themselves ensnared in an Iberian quagmire.

Conventional wisdom suggests that armies fight armies, a symphony of drilled movements on the canvas of the battlefield. Yet, in the Iberian Peninsula, the French found themselves combating not just the Spanish and Portuguese armies, but the very populace itself. The guerillas, civilian fighters that blended seamlessly into the background, fought a war of attrition, their skirmishes a constant drain on French resources and morale.

The Battle of Bailén in July 1808 stands as an epitome of the harsh realities the French faced. The French General Pierre Dupont, commanding a force of 20,000, was utterly defeated by General Francisco Castaños's Spanish army of 27,000. Bailén was a stark warning that the Iberian campaign would not be a straightforward affair. It was the first significant defeat for Napoleon's armies, shattering the illusion of French invincibility.

Roused by the plight of their Iberian allies, the British intervened under the leadership of Sir Arthur Wellesley, later the Duke of Wellington. Landing a British expeditionary force of 9,000 men in Portugal in August 1808, they quickly met the French at the Battle of Vimeiro. The British, despite their numerical inferiority, emerged victorious, pushing back the French forces and paving the way for the evacuation of Portugal.

This battle marked the first of many engagements between the British and French forces. The years to follow would witness a series of maneuvers, tactical retreats, and hard-fought battles. Wellington's strategic brilliance, coupled with the steadfast resistance of the Spanish and Portuguese, kept the French forces in a state of constant uncertainty.

The Battle of Talavera in 1809 stands as a testament to the intensity of the conflict. Here, a combined British and Spanish force of approximately 55,000 men, under the command of Wellesley and General Gregorio de la Cuesta, faced off against a French army of 46,000 under Joseph

Bonaparte and Marshal Jean-Baptiste Jourdan. The two-day battle ended with the British and Spanish retaining control of Talavera, further boosting the morale of the anti-French coalition.

The Peninsular War marked a departure from the norm, a brutal slog characterized by guerilla warfare and the indomitable spirit of the Spanish and Portuguese populace. The war was no longer confined to the battlefield; it permeated the very fabric of society, a shadow cast over the Iberian Peninsula.

Napoleon himself was compelled to intervene directly in 1808, leading a reinvigorated campaign to reassert French dominance. Yet, the 'Spanish Ulcer,' as he would later term it, proved stubbornly resistant to the French Emperor's cure. The occupation of Madrid and the installation of Joseph Bonaparte as the King of Spain did little to quell the resistance. Instead, it further ignited the flames of nationalistic fervor, turning the war into a struggle for Spanish independence.

In this crucible of conflict, the tactics employed by the British and their Spanish and Portuguese allies proved effective. The strategic retreat to the Lines of Torres Vedras in 1810, followed by the successful defense against Marshal André Masséna's French forces, marked a turning point in the war. The French were unable to breach the lines and were eventually forced to retreat, marking the beginning of the end for French ambitions in the Iberian Peninsula.

But the path to eventual victory was marred by hardship and atrocity. For the people of the Peninsula, the war was not only a fight for independence but a struggle for survival. The cost in human life was staggering. The conflict claimed an estimated 240,000 military lives on both sides. But the civilians paid an even higher price, with a death toll believed to exceed 500,000.

Yet, amidst the flames of war, the people of Spain and Portugal found their spirit of resistance. They fought not as disparate factions but as a united front, their combined might gradually turning the tide against French forces. This was a war that extended beyond the conventional boundaries of conflict, intertwining with the cultural and social fabric of the Iberian Peninsula. It was a war that transformed a people and reshaped a region, forever etched into the annals of history as a testament to the indomitable spirit of the Spanish and Portuguese people.

As for Napoleon, the Iberian quagmire proved to be a significant drain on his resources and a severe blow to his military reputation. The Peninsular War marked the beginning of his decline, a chapter of his life that served as a sobering reminder of the limits of power. This was Napoleon, the invincible conqueror, ensnared in a conflict that would become his Achilles' heel, a painful ulcer that never truly healed.

Chapter 16:

The Russian Campaign

In the annals of history, ambition has often been a double-edged sword, a beacon of progress and a harbinger of downfall. Few campaigns embody this paradox as vividly as Napoleon Bonaparte's ill-fated invasion of Russia in 1812. It was a venture as audacious as it was ill-conceived, a testament to the fatal allure of overreach and hubris.

As the summer of 1812 descended upon Europe, Napoleon was at the zenith of his power. His dominion stretched from the sun-kissed shores of Portugal to the snowy expanse of Poland. Yet, to the east lay a vast and enigmatic realm that resisted his influence – Russia. For Napoleon, the Tsar's refusal to adhere to the Continental System was a flagrant defiance that had to be dealt with.

The initial phases of the campaign saw Napoleon marshal an army of epic proportions. Named the Grande Armée, it was a sight to behold, a colossal force that numbered nearly half a million men at its peak. The troops were not just French but also comprised a cosmopolitan assortment of Poles, Italians, Germans, and a host of other nationalities from the French-controlled regions of Europe. As they marched towards the east, the sheer size of this force seemed to affirm

Napoleon's invincibility, a grand spectacle of power that appeared unbeatable.

Yet, beneath this awe-inspiring facade lay a gnawing uncertainty. Supply lines stretched thin across hostile terrains, a fact that would increasingly take its toll on the Grande Armée. Napoleon, ever the meticulous planner, had grossly underestimated the vastness of the Russian landscape and the logistical nightmare it posed.

As the Grande Armée delved deeper into Russian territory, the specter of battle loomed ahead. The Russians, led by Field Marshal Mikhail Kutuzov, employed a strategic retreat, systematically scorching their lands and leaving behind nothing but the smoldering remnants of a barren landscape. The tactic was simple yet devastatingly effective, designed to starve Napoleon's men and animals of sustenance. The absence of a decisive battle also slowly ate away at the morale of Napoleon's men, their enthusiasm waning as they trudged through the desolate landscape.

Finally, the stage was set for the Battle of Borodino on September 7, 1812. It was a clash of titans, the might of the Grande Armée pitted against the stalwart resistance of the Russian forces. Napoleon, typically a master of battlefield innovation, surprisingly opted for a direct and costly frontal assault, resulting in horrendous casualties on both sides.

Despite the high price, Napoleon managed to secure a pyrrhic victory, pushing the Russian forces to retreat. Yet, even in retreat, the Russians remained defiant, denying Napoleon the decisive capitulation he had hoped for. The path to Moscow lay open, but it was a hollow triumph, an empty city devoid of the spoils of war.

Napoleon entered Moscow expecting capitulation, a grand surrender that would cement his dominance. Instead, he found a city abandoned and devoid of supplies, soon to be swallowed by flames in a great fire. It was a scene from Dante's Inferno, a city consumed by fire, its empty streets echoing with the eerie silence of desolation.

The Russian winter was closing in, and Napoleon was left with little choice but to order a retreat. It was a bitter pill to swallow, the grand ambitions of conquest dissolving in the face of harsh reality. The retreat turned into a nightmare as the Russian winter took hold. Men and horses froze in the harsh cold, and those who survived faced constant harassment from Russian forces and partisans.

The scale of the disaster was staggering. Of the approximately 500,000 men who had started the campaign, fewer than 40,000 trudged back across the Niemen River, a mere shadow of the Grande Armée that had set out with such pomp and circumstance. It was a catastrophe on an unprecedented scale, an icy graveyard that bore silent testament to the costs of ambition.

The Russian Campaign was a turning point in Napoleon's saga. It revealed the cracks in the veneer of his invincibility and marked the beginning of the end of his reign. Yet, it was more than just a military disaster; it was a human tragedy on a massive scale, a poignant reminder of the terrible price of overreach.

The aftermath of the campaign left a deep scar on the collective psyche of Europe. Napoleon, the invincible conqueror, had faltered in the face of the Russian winter and the indomitable spirit of the Russian people. It was a sobering reality, a stark reminder that even the mightiest can stumble and that hubris often precedes a fall. Napoleon had flown too close to the sun, and like Icarus, he too had fallen.

Chapter 17:

Downfall and Exile

So has it ever been in the cruel theater of power, that a slight misstep can transform a hero into a pariah, a conqueror into an exile. This cruel truth was writ large in the life of Napoleon Bonaparte, the French ruler whose fortunes, once so dazzling, crumbled under the relentless wheel of time.

It was 1813, a year after the disastrous Russian campaign, and Europe was no longer the chessboard on which Napoleon could maneuver at will. The Grand Armée, once the terror of the continent, was now a pale shadow of its former self, bled dry by the merciless Russian winter and ceaseless conflict.

Across the breadth of Europe, Napoleon's enemies, long chafing under the French yoke, began to stir. Seeing the lion wounded, they sensed an opportunity. The Sixth Coalition formed, an alliance of powers that included Britain, Russia, Prussia, Sweden, and Austria, among others. Their objective was singular and unwavering: to break Napoleon's stranglehold on Europe.

Under these gathering clouds, Napoleon did what he did best: he fought. With a hastily assembled army of young and inexperienced soldiers—dubbed Marie-Louise's by the

French public, in a poignant reference to the young men, barely older than Napoleon's own son—Bonaparte marched into battle.

The War of the Sixth Coalition was marked by a series of clashes that saw the balance of power teeter precariously. Notably, the Battle of Lützen in May 1813 showcased Napoleon's military genius, as he led his unseasoned troops to an unlikely victory. Yet, the absence of his seasoned veterans was keenly felt, and every victory seemed to exact an exorbitant price in blood.

The pivotal moment came at the Battle of Leipzig, often referred to as the Battle of the Nations, in October 1813. This was warfare on a grand scale, a titanic clash involving over half a million men. The odds were heavily stacked against Napoleon; he commanded a force of about 200,000 against a Coalition army that numbered over 300,000.

True to his nature, Napoleon launched a series of ferocious attacks, hoping to fracture the Allied forces before they could consolidate their superior numbers. He sought to recreate the battlefield brilliance of his earlier years, aiming his forces at the heart of the enemy. Yet, the Allied forces, under the experienced stewardship of Tsar Alexander I, Field Marshal Karl von Schwarzenberg, and Crown Prince Charles John of Sweden, managed to absorb the French onslaught.

After four days of intense fighting, the outcome was clear. Napoleon's forces, outnumbered and exhausted, were driven out of Leipzig in a large scale retreat. It was a major blow, signaling that the balance of power had irrevocably shifted. The eagle, it seemed, had finally been caged.

As the Allies pressed their advantage, they advanced into France early in 1814. Despite Napoleon's desperate attempts to resist, Paris was captured in March, a severe psychological blow to the Emperor. Under immense pressure, and facing the loss of political support, Napoleon abdicated the throne on April 6, 1814, in favor of his son, Napoleon II. The Allies, however, refused to accept the young boy as ruler, forcing Napoleon to abdicate unconditionally a few days later.

The whirlwind that had swept across Europe finally seemed to have spent its force, and Napoleon, the man at its eye, was sent into exile on the Mediterranean island of Elba. The conditions of his exile were generous; he was given sovereignty over the island and allowed to retain a small military force. Yet, for a man who had held sway over much of Europe, it was a bitter comedown. The Emperor had become an outcast, the ruler of a tiny island.

From his villa on Elba, Napoleon could gaze across the sea towards the France he had shaped with his ambition and audacity. He was only 46 years old, and he had already reached the end of his journey—or so it seemed. Yet, the fire that had driven him to the heights of power was not entirely extinguished. As he stared across the wine-dark sea, one can imagine him dreaming of another chance, another roll of the dice.

Thus ended a chapter in the extraordinary life of Napoleon Bonaparte. The man who had risen from obscurity to rule an empire found himself diminished and dispossessed, cast away on an island in the Mediterranean. It was a testament to the vicissitudes of fortune, a stark reminder that even the greatest of us are not immune to downfall. Yet, even in defeat, Napoleon remained a figure of fascination, a symbol of the dual nature of ambition and power, their ability to lift us to the heavens and then dash us to the ground. The twilight of the eagle had arrived, and yet, his story was far from over.

Chapter 18:

The Hundred Days

As our story twists its way through the labyrinth of history, we find Napoleon, not languishing in a prison cell or laid low in ignominy, but thriving on a tiny Mediterranean island of Elba. But there is only so much a man like Napoleon can bear. An island of six thousand souls is too paltry a stage for a man who once presided over an empire.

Barely ten months into his exile, the humdrum island life began to gnaw at Napoleon. To the man who once commanded the allegiance of millions, this island existence was intolerable. The theater of history beckoned, and he was poised to make a return. A daring escape was planned, not from a fortress but from the entire world's gaze.

On February 26, 1815, in a stroke of audacious bravura that even by Napoleon's standards was ambitious, he slipped away from his island exile. Seven hundred men, the remnants of his loyal Imperial Guard, joined him aboard the brig Inconstant. With the wind in their sails and destiny as their compass, they set course for France.

Napoleon's arrival on the mainland was greeted with apprehension by some, jubilation by others. The eagle had landed at Golfe-Juan, and the news spread through France like a summer wildfire. As he commenced his journey towards Paris, the remaining royalist troops stationed to arrest him instead joined his ranks, swelling his forces. The old magic, it seemed, had not entirely dissipated. The specter of a man declared 'the Enemy of Europe' by the Vienna Congress was once again marching on Paris, his ambition burning brighter than ever.

On March 20, 1815, Napoleon entered Paris, not as a conqueror but as a liberator, greeted by joyous crowds. The reigning King Louis XVIII had already fled, leaving the city—and the country—for Napoleon to reclaim. Within a span of a mere three weeks, the exiled ruler had become the Emperor of the French again, a feat of political resurrection unrivaled in modern history. These were the opening scenes of what would come to be known as 'The Hundred Days'—a period of frantic activity, which, for its sheer dynamism and dramatic intensity, bears little comparison in the annals of history.

Once in power, Napoleon undertook a series of reforms aimed at placating his opponents and securing his grip on power. He proposed a new constitution, termed 'Acte additionnel aux constitutions de l'Empire', promising more civil liberties and better representation. It was a bid for popular support, a social contract that embodied the lessons of his past.

He also sought to reassure the major European powers. He penned letters to the monarchs of Austria, Britain, and

Russia, expressing his desire for peace. In his letter to the Prince Regent of Britain, he wrote, "After presenting the spectacle of great campaigns to the world, from now on it will be more pleasant to know of no other rivalry than that of the benefits of peace, of no other struggle than the holy conflict of the happiness of peoples." Napoleon, it appeared, had been transformed into a peaceful ruler, a lamb dressed in an eagle's feathers.

But the winds of change that had carried Napoleon back to power were not to blow in his favor for long. The Allied powers at the Vienna Congress declared him an outlaw. A 'monster', a 'disturber of the world's peace', he was to be banished, and the sanctity of the European map was to be preserved. War, it seemed, was inevitable.

Yet, even as clouds of conflict gathered, Napoleon proved himself a master of the domestic sphere. He moved quickly to consolidate his authority, to rally the people and the army around him. The machinery of government, which had rusted under the Bourbons, was set into motion again. Tax reforms were implemented, public works initiated, and the National Guard reinstated. It was as though Napoleon was trying to compress a decade of administration into a mere hundred days.

The Hundred Days period was marked by ceaseless activity, as Napoleon, with his back against the wall, tried to outmaneuver his opponents at every turn. He summoned the 'Champ de Mai', a massive assembly, to proclaim the new constitution. He began to rebuild his army, drawing upon veterans of his previous campaigns. The imperial machinery was set into motion, with Napoleon at the helm, guiding it with his indomitable will.

But for all his fervor, the deck was stacked against him. The Allied powers, sensing the imminent threat posed by Napoleon, put aside their differences. Britain, Prussia, Austria, and Russia pledged to dedicate 150,000 men each to defeat Napoleon and pledged to keep their coalition until he was definitively overthrown. The Congress of Vienna had effectively become a war council, with the singular goal of defeating Napoleon.

In this period of a hundred days, Napoleon had risen from the ashes of his past, only to find himself on the brink of an even greater precipice. The wheel of fortune, which had once lifted him to the height of power, was now primed to hurl him into the abyss. Yet, undeterred, he steeled himself for the trials to come.

In the annals of history, the Hundred Days stand out as a period of intense drama, marked by high stakes and higher ambitions. It was a moment in time when the indomitable spirit of one man threatened to overturn the world order. Napoleon, the prodigal son of destiny, had returned, bringing with him the tumultuous winds of change. Whether he would weather the storm or be swept away by it—that was a question only time could answer.

Chapter 19:

The Field of Waterloo

On June 16, 1815, a blanket of brooding uncertainty spread over the undulating fields of Belgium. The ground beneath, etched with furrows sown by farmers, was destined to be ploughed afresh, not by the humble ploughshares but by the cruel heels of war. The approaching storm, laden with the might of clashing empires, would turn this verdant expanse into the fabled battlefield of Waterloo.

On one side stood Napoleon Bonaparte, the phoenix of Europe, once again at the helm of the French Empire, leading an army of about 73,000 seasoned men. Opposite him, the newly minted alliance—the Seventh Coalition—marshaled their forces under the command of Arthur Wellesley, the Duke of Wellington. A highly regarded military tactician, Wellington led a mixed force of around 68,000 men, primarily composed of British, Dutch, and German soldiers, with the Prussian army under Gebhard Leberecht von Blücher supporting from the east.

The battle was not merely a contest of military strength but a struggle of contrasting ideologies and national imperatives. As the dawn of June 18, 1815, broke over the

Belgian countryside, the stage was set for an epic confrontation, a finale to the Napoleonic era.

The day started with deceptive tranquility. Napoleon, always the early riser, was unusually complacent that morning. Surveying the battlefield from his command post on a small knoll near the farm of La Belle Alliance, he braced himself for what he believed to be a definitive victory. The French artillery, comprising 250 guns, lay silent, awaiting the order to rend the morning air. In his mind, Napoleon saw the familiar patterns of success—first a heavy artillery bombardment, then a decisive cavalry charge, and finally, the steady march of his indomitable infantry.

Opposite him, Wellington, ever the pragmatist, had chosen his ground meticulously. With his headquarters at the inn of Mont-Saint-Jean, he organized his forces along a ridge, with the farmhouses of La Haye Sainte, Hougoumont, and Papelotte fortified as strong points. These positions provided his troops with a protective shield against the French artillery and a base from which to launch counterattacks.

Napoleon initiated the battle around 11:30 am, with a diversionary attack on Hougoumont farm, held by the British Guards. The attack, meant to draw Wellington's reserves to the southern flank, soon escalated into a bitter fight for control. The stubborn defense of the farm by the British tied down a significant portion of the French forces, inadvertently thwarting Napoleon's initial plan.

Meanwhile, to the east of the battlefield, Marshal Ney, Napoleon's trusted subordinate, was preparing for the main assault. At 1:30 pm, the deafening roar of French cannons shattered the midday calm. An intense artillery bombardment began, followed by the advance of Napoleon's infantry toward Wellington's center, targeting La Haye Sainte.

The British line stood firm under the assault, returning fire with their disciplined volleys. The farm of La Haye Sainte turned into a battleground, with control passing between the French and the Allies several times. But the tide turned in favor of the Allies when the Prussian forces, led by Blücher, began to arrive on the eastern flank of the battlefield. Their timely intervention put additional pressure on the French forces, forcing them to divide their attention.

Ney, in an attempt to seize the initiative, launched a series of cavalry charges against the British center. However, the British infantry, trained to withstand cavalry attacks, formed into defensive squares. The French cavalry, like waves breaking on a rocky shore, crashed against these squares only to be repulsed each time.

As the day waned, the situation began to look dire for Napoleon. With his forces stretched thin and his strategies faltering, he decided to commit his elite Imperial Guard to the battle. This was his last roll of the dice, a desperate bid to break the stubborn British line.

Around 7:30 pm, the tall bearskin caps of the Imperial Guard emerged from the smoke and gunpowder haze. A sense of dread fell over the battlefield as these veterans, who had never known defeat, advanced toward the Allied line. Wellington, recognizing the gravity of the moment, personally oversaw the repositioning of his troops to repel the assault.

The ensuing clash was fierce, but the Allied forces, bolstered by fresh Prussian troops, managed to hold their ground. As the sun began to set, a cheer went up from the Allied line—"La Garde recule!"—the Guard retreats! This was the first time the Imperial Guard had been forced to retreat, and the psychological impact on the French troops was devastating. Seeing the Guard falter, panic spread through the French ranks, transforming their orderly retreat into a rout.

Wellington, seizing the moment, gave the order that echoed through the ages, "The day is ours. Go at them, in God's name!" The Allied forces surged forward, turning the French retreat into a complete rout. Napoleon, once the master of Europe, fled the battlefield, his dreams of empire shattered on the fields of Waterloo.

The Battle of Waterloo was a thunderous finale to Napoleon's rule. It was not just the tactical acumen of Wellington or the timely intervention of Blücher that won the day. It was also the resolve of the Allied soldiers who stood their ground in the face of overwhelming odds, the endurance of the men defending Hougoumont and La Haye Sainte, the discipline of the British infantry squares, and the heroism of individual soldiers.

As the smoke cleared over the devastated fields of Waterloo, the cost of the day's events became apparent. Nearly 25,000 Frenchmen lay dead or wounded, along with about 22,000 Allied casualties. The fields, once lush and green, were now a tableau of human tragedy.

Waterloo marked the end of Napoleon's dream of a revived French Empire, but its impact extended far beyond the immediate political and military outcomes. The thunder of cannons had faded, and the smoke had cleared, but the echoes of Waterloo would reverberate through the corridors of time, shaping the destiny of nations and individuals alike. The Battle of Waterloo wasn't just a clash of armies; it was a collision of destinies, a fulcrum upon which the course of European history pivoted.

Chapter 20:

Second Exile and Death

On June 22, 1815, the specter of Waterloo and its devastating defeat hung heavily over the once invincible Napoleon Bonaparte. The man who had dominated the European stage with audacious might and steely resolve now found himself beaten, broken. That day, he signed his second abdication in the grand, ornate chamber of the Elysée Palace, a mere shadow of his former imperial majesty.

His ultimate fate lay thousands of miles away on a tiny speck of land in the South Atlantic: Saint Helena. Even the name of the island seemed to echo with a dirge-like quality. Banished to this remote outpost by the British, Napoleon's world shrank from grand palaces and fields of battle to a damp, draughty house nestled in a verdant valley aptly named Longwood.

Life at Longwood was a far cry from the glamour and grandeur of Napoleon's heyday. Gone were the stately halls and opulent feasts of the Tuileries, replaced by an existence marked by dampness, solitude, and the constant nagging of a cold Atlantic wind. Here, in this remote outpost of Empire,

Napoleon Bonaparte, Emperor of the French, Conqueror of Europe, met his twilight years.

Longwood was not a prison in the traditional sense, but its insular isolation proved a far more formidable cage than any bars or shackles. Cut off from the world, Napoleon lived under the constant surveillance of Sir Hudson Lowe, the British governor appointed to ensure that the fallen emperor remained firmly sequestered.

Their relationship was contentious at best, with Napoleon chafing under Lowe's stringent security measures. The governor, on his part, viewed his charge with a certain cold detachment, carrying out his duties with all the unwavering dedication of a dutiful civil servant.

Napoleon's days on Saint Helena were marked by a monotonous routine. He would often spend his mornings reading or writing, his afternoons taking solitary walks or gardening. Despite the somber setting, he was not entirely alone. A few loyal companions had accompanied him into exile, providing him with a semblance of his old court.

It was during these long, languorous hours that Napoleon began crafting his memoirs. Poring over the details of his life and campaigns, he sought to control his narrative, to ensure that his legacy would not be shaped by his enemies.

His health, however, began to deteriorate. He suffered from bouts of stomach pain and swelling, fatigue, and a noticeable loss of weight. The once-vibrant conqueror was steadily reduced to a frail, ill man. Despite the presence of his personal physician, Barry O'Meara, his condition worsened over time.

Amid his suffering, Napoleon maintained his fiery spirit, refusing to be defeated by his circumstances. He filled his time with intellectual pursuits, engaging in lively discussions with his companions, reading extensively, and even teaching himself English. The flame of the emperor, it seemed, could not be entirely extinguished.

His last days, however, were filled with agony. The man who had led armies and commanded the destiny of nations was reduced to an invalid, confined to his bed. Despite the constant care of his companions and physicians, Napoleon's condition continued to deteriorate.

Finally, on May 5, 1821, as a storm lashed the island, Napoleon Bonaparte breathed his last. The cause of his death was officially recorded as stomach cancer, but the specter of possible arsenic poisoning would later cloud the circumstances surrounding his demise, fueling speculation and controversy that endure to this day.

In the end, the Emperor was laid to rest in a tomb under two willow trees near a spring in the Geranium Valley, a peaceful, idyllic spot that was far removed from the grandeur of his former life. Inscribed on his tombstone was simply "Napoleon." No imperial titles, no grand epithets - just the name of the man who had once held Europe in his grasp.

However, the final act of Napoleon's life was yet to be played. In 1840, under the reign of King Louis-Philippe, Napoleon's remains were exhumed and returned to France, the country he had once ruled with an iron hand. In a grand state funeral, his body was interred in the grandiose surroundings of Les Invalides, finally finding rest in the nation that he had shaped, for better or worse.

The story of Napoleon Bonaparte, from the dusty streets of Corsica to the echoing halls of power in Paris, and finally to the desolate windswept bluffs of Saint Helena, is one marked by a relentless drive for power, a boundless ambition, and an unquenchable thirst for glory. However, his final years of exile paint a different picture of the man. They show a Napoleon stripped of power and grandeur, a man wrestling with his legacy, grappling with his past, and confronting his mortality.

Yet, even in his isolation, even in his diminishing health, Napoleon did not yield. He wrote, he debated, he instructed, he questioned - and in doing so, he left behind an indelible imprint on history. In his final years, Napoleon Bonaparte was not the invincible Emperor, the awe-inspiring General, or the shrewd statesman. He was a man, perhaps more human in his frailty and solitude than he had ever been in his power and glory. And it is in this humanity that we find the true measure of his life.

Chapter 21:

Napoleon and the French Society

Napoleon Bonaparte, the once-swaggering conqueror whose specter still looms large over the annals of history, lived a life that was anything but ordinary. Yet, it was not the battlefield but the quieter, more deliberate theater of societal transformation where Napoleon enacted some of his most enduring legacies. His relationship with French society – and the profound impact he had upon it – provides a lens through which to view the man himself. More than just a military genius, he was a reformer, a shaper of nations, and a creator of a modern state.

The France that Napoleon inherited as First Consul in 1799 was a nation transformed by the turmoil of the Revolution. The old regime, with its rigid hierarchy and privilege, was swept away in a wave of radical fervor, replaced by an ideological commitment to liberty, equality, and fraternity. Yet, the nascent Republic was riven with internal strife, its promise of democratic utopia increasingly overshadowed by the bloody reality of the Reign of Terror.

Napoleon stepped into this turbulent maelstrom with a promise of stability and order. He was a son of the Revolution, shaped by its ideals, yet he was also a pragmatist, recognizing the need for strong, central authority. Under his firm hand, France began to emerge from the shadow of revolutionary chaos into a structured, modern state.

One of Napoleon's first acts was the establishment of a centralized, bureaucratic government. This was a sharp break from the feudal structure that had dominated France for centuries, where power was dispersed amongst the nobility. Instead, Napoleon created a cadre of civil servants, a "new nobility" based not on birth, but on merit. These men, drawn from all classes of society, were the wheels and cogs of his new administrative machine.

In a society scarred by the class struggles of the Revolution, this meritocratic principle was revolutionary. It promised social mobility, an opportunity for talented individuals from all walks of life to rise to prominence. This was not mere tokenism; many of the men who served under Napoleon, from his marshals to his ministers, were of humble origin, their rise testament to Napoleon's commitment to meritocracy.

But Napoleon's vision extended beyond the structures of governance. He recognized that for France to flourish, it needed to harness the intellectual and creative potential of its citizens. Under his patronage, schools and universities were established across the nation, fostering a culture of learning and intellectualism. Education was reformed, standardized curriculums were introduced, and an emphasis was placed on the sciences and modern languages.

For women, however, Napoleon's France offered little in the way of progress. The ideals of the Revolution had hinted at the possibility of greater gender equality, but under Napoleon, women found themselves firmly relegated to traditional roles. His Napoleonic Code, widely hailed as a landmark legal reform, enshrined a patriarchal model of family, restricting women's rights and reinforcing their status as dependents of their fathers or husbands.

Despite his strides in modernizing French society, Napoleon's relationship with the Church was complex. The Revolution had seen a violent backlash against the Catholic Church, with many of its lands seized and clergy persecuted. Yet, Napoleon, ever the pragmatist, recognized the political and social utility of religion. In 1801, he signed the Concordat with the Pope, restoring the Catholic Church as the majority religion of France while also ensuring its subservience to the state.

This balancing act between tradition and modernity was a defining characteristic of Napoleon's approach to societal reform. On one hand, he embraced the radical ideals of the Revolution, pushing through reforms that dismantled feudal structures and championed meritocracy. On the other, he sought to bring back a sense of order and stability, restoring elements of the old regime and the Church, even as he bent them to his will.

Yet, one cannot discuss Napoleon's impact on French society without acknowledging the darker side of his rule. His lust for power led him to undermine the very principles of democracy that the Revolution had fought for. While he styled himself as the "protector of the Revolution", he dismantled the Republic, establishing an authoritarian regime that concentrated power in his hands.

His use of propaganda, his manipulation of the press, and his suppression of political dissent were tools of control that would later be echoed by autocrats throughout history. While Napoleon brought order and stability to France, he did so at the cost of liberty, using the machinery of the state to maintain his grip on power.

Yet, for all its contradictions, Napoleon's France was a nation transformed. His vision of a centralized, meritocratic society laid the groundwork for the modern French state. His educational reforms fostered a culture of learning and intellectualism that would see France become a beacon of culture and arts. His legal reforms, most notably the Napoleonic Code, would shape French law for generations to come.

Even his more controversial acts, such as his relationship with the Church and his suppression of women's rights, reveal much about the societal norms of the time and offer a rich field for historical inquiry. Through it all, Napoleon's influence was indelible, leaving a mark on French society that is still visible today.

Napoleon Bonaparte, once the scourge of Europe, the invincible general, was also Napoleon the reformer, the statesman, the creator of a modern state. In his life, he held many roles - hero, villain, conqueror, and emperor. Yet, it was in his impact on French society that we see a different side of Napoleon, one that continues to resonate in the heart and soul of France.

Chapter 22:

The Napoleonic Legend

In the grand theater of history, few characters command the stage with as much force and flamboyance as Napoleon Bonaparte. He was a man who fashioned an era in his own image, and in doing so, etched an indelible mark on the pages of time. Yet, for all his tangible accomplishments, it is perhaps in the realm of myth and memory that Napoleon's most enduring legacy lies. He was not simply a master of the battlefield, but also of the narrative, crafting an image and a legend that continues to captivate the world even two centuries after his death.

From the moment he burst onto the political stage in the aftermath of the French Revolution, Napoleon demonstrated an acute understanding of the power of mythmaking. He recognized that history is often a tale told by the victors, and he resolved to be the author of his own story. In the swirling chaos of Revolutionary France, he cast himself as the savior of the republic, the steadfast hero who could steer the nation through its darkest hour.

In Napoleon's hands, every victory was not merely a military triumph, but a chapter in a grand narrative, a testament to his genius and the destiny of France. His campaigns were framed as epic quests, his battles as clashes of titans. Through his bulletins and proclamations, he painted vivid pictures of his exploits, imbuing them with a sense of drama and inevitability that captured the public imagination. The Battle of Austerlitz was not just a strategic masterpiece, but a "sun of Austerlitz" that shone brightly on the French empire.

Yet, Napoleon's self-mythologizing extended beyond his military endeavors. He fashioned himself as a modern Caesar, a visionary leader who could drag France out of the ashes of the Revolution and usher in an age of glory and prosperity. His rule was marked by grand gestures and symbols that reinforced this image. The adoption of the imperial eagle, the construction of grand monuments and boulevards in Paris, and, of course, his self-coronation as emperor were all designed to project an aura of grandeur and invincibility.

But the creation of a myth is not simply about the crafting of a grand narrative. It is also about controlling the narrative, and here too, Napoleon proved to be a master. He cultivated a loyal cadre of artists and writers who churned out a steady stream of propaganda that glorified his rule. He exercised tight control over the press, ensuring that his exploits were reported in the most favorable light. Dissenting voices were ruthlessly suppressed, and his critics were often exiled or imprisoned.

Yet, even as he fashioned his own legend, Napoleon also became the subject of popular myths and folklore. His extraordinary rise from obscure Corsican origins to the pinnacle of power inspired countless tales and anecdotes, some of them bordering on the fantastical. He was said to have supernatural powers, to be able to control the weather, to possess a "star of destiny" that guided his fortunes. These stories, often spread by word of mouth, added another layer to the Napoleonic myth, elevating him to a near-mythical figure in the public imagination.

It is worth noting, however, that the Napoleonic legend was not uniformly positive. In the lands that he conquered and the nations that he antagonized, Napoleon was often cast as a villain, a tyrant who trampled on liberties in his quest for power. In Britain, he was caricatured as a short, petulant despot, a figure of ridicule rather than fear. His disastrous Russian campaign and his ultimate defeat at Waterloo further tarnished his image, transforming him from a seemingly invincible conqueror to a fallen Icarus.

But, in a strange twist of fate, it was in his downfall and exile that Napoleon's legend truly took on a life of its own. Cut off from the world on the remote island of Saint Helena, Napoleon had one final opportunity to shape his legacy. Through his memoirs and conversations with his captors, he presented a narrative of his life and career that was rich in self-justification and revisionism. He portrayed himself as a champion of the French people, a defender of the Revolution's ideals, and a victim of a coalition of monarchies that feared the spread of republicanism.

This narrative, presented with the dramatic flair that had been Napoleon's trademark, found a receptive audience. In the decades that followed his death, the Napoleonic legend grew in stature. He was resurrected as a romantic hero, a tragic figure who, for all his flaws, had dared to challenge the established order and dream of a united Europe. His tomb at Les Invalides became a place of pilgrimage, his life and deeds the subject of countless books, paintings, and later, films.

In the end, the Napoleonic legend is a testament to the power of mythmaking, a masterclass in the art of narrative control. It is a testament to the enduring allure of the individual in history, the figure who, through sheer force of will and personality, can shape the world in their image. And it is a reminder that history, as much as it is about facts and dates, is also about stories and perceptions.

Today, the figure of Napoleon continues to loom large in the collective imagination. He is a symbol of French national pride, a beacon of military genius, and a reminder of the perils of unchecked ambition. His legend, like the man himself, is a complex tapestry, woven from strands of truth, exaggeration, and outright fabrication. But, in its complexity and contradictions, it captures the essence of the man and the era he embodied – a time of tumultuous change, grand ambitions, and a dream of glory that, for a brief moment, set the world ablaze.

Chapter 23:

Contemporary Views

In the shimmering heat of the Egyptian desert, a man cast a long, distinct shadow. The shadow belonged to Napoleon Bonaparte, a figure who, even in his lifetime, cast an equally compelling shadow over the world. The silhouettes and nuances of this shadow, like the shifting sands of Egypt, formed the contemporary views of Napoleon, a mélange of praise, criticism, awe, and resentment.

Through the prism of these contemporary perspectives, we glimpse Napoleon not as a monolithic figure of history, but as a flesh and blood human being, inspiring a spectrum of responses from his allies, enemies, and observers.

For his most ardent supporters, Napoleon was a savior, the harbinger of a new era of French greatness. His admirers saw in him a dynamic leader who rose from the ashes of a revolution to guide France into a period of unparalleled glory. One of the greatest admirers was his personal secretary, Louis Antoine Fauvelet de Bourrienne, who had known Napoleon since their school days in Brienne.

To Bourrienne, Napoleon was an awe-inspiring figure, a "human comet" that illuminated the political landscape.

Bourrienne wrote of Napoleon's "great mind, profound cunning, correct judgment, and rapid conception," and noted his tireless work ethic. To him, the Corsican was a heroic figure, a "child of destiny" who had seized his fate with both hands and carved an empire out of the chaos of revolution.

Then there were those who admired Napoleon for his legal and administrative reforms. Jean Jacques Régis de Cambacérès, the Second Consul, was instrumental in drafting the Napoleonic Code and saw Napoleon as a revolutionary reformer. He praised Napoleon's ability to establish stability and order and admired his insistence on the rule of law.

Yet, within this choir of praise, there were dissenting voices, those who viewed Napoleon through a less flattering lens. To them, he was not a hero or a reformer, but a tyrant, a dictator, a self-proclaimed emperor who had betrayed the ideals of the Revolution. Among these critics, the most vocal was perhaps Madame de Staël, a woman of letters and a key figure in French literary circles.

Exiled from Paris for her outspoken views, de Staël viewed Napoleon as a despot, a "sun that gives light but no warmth." She deplored his autocratic rule and the curtailment of civil liberties under his regime. She also critiqued his thirst for power, claiming that "his will to power is the entire man."

In England, the land of his greatest enemy, views of Napoleon were predominantly negative. Here he was often caricatured as "Boney," a bogeyman who threatened the peace and stability of Europe. Sir Walter Scott, the Scottish novelist, wrote a nine-volume biography of Napoleon that portrayed him as a military genius but also as a ruthless tyrant. To Scott, Napoleon's military achievements were undeniable, but they were overshadowed by his insatiable hunger for power and his disregard for the human cost of his wars.

Among the monarchs of Europe, Napoleon was largely viewed with fear and suspicion. They saw him as an upstart, a revolutionary who threatened the established order. The Austrian Emperor Francis II referred to him as "the most dangerous man in Europe," while Tsar Alexander I of Russia, once a tentative ally, grew to view Napoleon as a personal nemesis, an embodiment of unchecked ambition and imperialistic expansionism.

Even within his own family, views of Napoleon were mixed. His brothers, who owed their elevated statuses to Napoleon's generosity, often grumbled about his domineering nature. His brother Lucien, a staunch republican, clashed with Napoleon over his decision to crown himself emperor and eventually broke with him, refusing to support what he saw as a betrayal of republican principles.

In the broader spectrum of contemporary views, we see reflections of Napoleon's complex persona, his monumental achievements, and his flaws. Napoleon, as seen by his contemporaries, is a man of contrasts, a figure of immense talent and ambition, but also a leader whose pursuit of personal glory often eclipsed the values he claimed to uphold.

In understanding these views, we begin to grasp the magnitude of Napoleon's impact on his contemporaries, an impact that reverberated across national borders, social classes, and ideological divides. These views, however, are not simply historical artifacts, fossilized impressions of a bygone era. They are, in many ways, the seeds of the Napoleonic legend, the raw materials from which future generations would construct their understanding of Napoleon.

As we navigate the labyrinth of contemporary perspectives, we encounter Napoleon the hero and Napoleon the villain, Napoleon the reformer and Napoleon the tyrant, Napoleon the unstoppable conqueror and Napoleon the fallen Icarus. Each of these faces of Napoleon offers a facet of truth, a piece of the puzzle that makes up the man and the myth.

In the final analysis, the contemporary views of Napoleon illuminate not only the man himself, but also the age he lived in. They underscore the transformative nature of his rule, the polarizing effect of his personality, and the profound impact he had on the people of his time. Whether viewed as a hero or a villain, a savior or a despot, Napoleon, to his contemporaries, was an undeniable force, a man who, for better or for worse, had etched his name on the canvas of history in bold, indelible strokes.

Chapter 24:

Napoleon and Europe

It was as if an invisible hand had descended upon the political map of Europe, smudging the old lines and etching new ones. The hand belonged to Napoleon Bonaparte, a man who, in a matter of years, had rewritten the political lexicon of an entire continent. But what was the nature of Napoleon's influence on Europe, and how did it shape the continent's political geography and national identities?

Napoleon's impact on Europe was like a meteor strike, both destructive and transformative. The wave of changes unleashed by Napoleon's rule rippled far beyond the borders of France, reshaping the political, social, and cultural landscapes of Europe in profound and lasting ways.

Within the imperial confines of his rule, Napoleon implemented a series of reforms that significantly transformed the nations under his influence. Central among these was the promotion of meritocracy over hereditary privilege. In regions like Italy, Holland, and the Germanic territories, positions of power were no longer reserved for the aristocracy. Talented individuals, regardless of their social backgrounds, could ascend the ladders of power based on their abilities.

The introduction of the Napoleonic Code, France's civil law code, to the annexed territories was another transformative aspect of Napoleon's European influence. This code reformed the justice system by providing a unified set of laws that prioritized individual rights, property rights, and secularism, replacing a patchwork of traditional laws and customs that often perpetuated inequality and feudal privilege.

Napoleon's influence was not limited to legal and administrative reforms. He also brought about infrastructural development in the territories under his rule. Roads, bridges, and canals were constructed, facilitating trade and communication. Schools were established, promoting literacy and education. These measures contributed to the modernization and development of these regions.

Yet, Napoleon's Europe was not a landscape of unblemished progress. The imposition of French authority often ignited resistance, leading to brutal reprisals. The demands of war and the requirement to supply French troops led to widespread resentment among the local populations. The imposition of the Continental System, a trade embargo against Britain, wreaked economic havoc in many parts of Europe.

The German states, which had been consolidated into the Confederation of the Rhine under Napoleon's watch, exemplify these contradictions. While the French occupation brought about administrative efficiency, legal reforms, and infrastructural improvements, it also stirred German nationalism, ultimately culminating in the Wars of Liberation against the French rule.

In Spain, Napoleon's attempt to install his brother Joseph as king ignited the Peninsular War, a conflict marked by guerrilla warfare, brutal atrocities, and widespread destruction. The war not only drained Napoleon's resources but also kindled the flames of Spanish nationalism and precipitated the eventual downfall of the Napoleonic Empire.

Similarly, in Italy, while French rule brought about administrative reforms and the abolition of feudal privileges, it also stirred the currents of Italian nationalism. The ideals of the French Revolution and the practices of the Napoleonic rule left a lasting imprint on the Italian political consciousness, planting the seeds of the Risorgimento, the movement for Italian unification.

But it is perhaps in the shifting borders of Europe that we see the most vivid evidence of Napoleon's influence. From the creation of the Confederation of the Rhine and the Grand Duchy of Warsaw to the annexation of territories in Italy and the dissolution of the Holy Roman Empire, Napoleon redrew the map of Europe, transforming its political geography in ways that would reverberate through the subsequent centuries.

Yet, as his empire expanded, so did the coalition of forces against him. From Russia to Austria, Britain to Prussia, the European powers united in their opposition to Napoleon's hegemonic ambitions, leading to a series of wars that consumed the continent. The result was a Europe steeped in conflict and upheaval, a continent molded and marred by the force of Napoleon's ambitions.

Through the crucible of conflict, a new European consciousness began to take shape, one marked by heightened nationalism and a shared opposition to French dominance. In a paradoxical twist, Napoleon, the emperor of the French, the architect of a European empire, became a catalyst for the emergence of modern European nation-states.

In assessing Napoleon's influence on Europe, one must tread carefully on a landscape marked by shifting sands, a landscape of contradictions and complexities. On one hand, Napoleon stands as a transformative figure who brought about sweeping reforms, promoted meritocracy, and modernized the nations under his rule. On the other hand, he emerges as a figure of conflict and domination, whose imperial ambitions ignited wars, sparked nationalism, and altered the political geography of Europe.

At its core, the story of Napoleon and Europe is a narrative of power and transformation, of destruction and renewal. It is a narrative that reveals the indelible imprint of one man's ambition on the canvas of a continent. It underscores the dialectic of history, the interplay of action and reaction, of progress and backlash, of unity and division.

Ultimately, Napoleon's influence on Europe cannot be contained within the neat borders of praise or condemnation. It must be understood within the expansive landscape of history, a landscape marked by the interplay of light and shadow, a landscape forever altered by the footsteps of a man named Napoleon Bonaparte.

Chapter 25:

The Napoleonic Code

In the annals of human history, few have left a legacy as enduring and impactful as Napoleon Bonaparte. The echoes of his battles still resonate in the historical consciousness, his political strategies continue to be dissected in scholarly circles, and his personal life remains a subject of enduring fascination. Yet, among all the aspects of Napoleon's legacy, one stands out for its breadth of influence and the depth of its impact: the Napoleonic Code.

The Napoleonic Code, or the Civil Code of the French, enacted in 1804, was the cornerstone of Napoleon's legal reforms. It was a legal superstructure designed to bring order to the chaos of post-revolutionary France and to institutionalize the principles of the Revolution within a framework of law. It was the embodiment of Napoleon's ambition to create a modern, rational system of law that would be the bedrock of French society and administration.

As we navigate the complex terrains of this legal masterpiece, it is essential to comprehend the context within which it was born. The Revolution had razed the old regime's institutions to the ground, leaving behind a vacuum. In this milieu of legal uncertainty and societal instability, Napoleon, then First Consul, recognized the need for a comprehensive, rational code of laws. He aimed to create a legal code that would sweep away the vestiges of the old regime and enshrine the revolutionary principles of equality, personal freedom, and property rights.

To achieve this monumental task, Napoleon assembled a commission of four esteemed jurists: Tronchet, Maleville, Portalis, and Bigot de Préameneu. For Napoleon, this was not a project to be relegated to the sidelines. He took an active role in the drafting of the Code, participating in 57 out of the 102 meetings of the drafting commission, engaging in heated debates, and molding the Code with his vision.

The Napoleonic Code was a legal edifice of stunning simplicity and clarity. It was designed to be understood by the ordinary citizen, eschewing the obscurity and complexity that characterized pre-revolutionary French law. The Code was divided into three books, each focusing on a particular aspect of civil law: persons, property, and different ways of acquiring property.

The Code was a potent symbol of legal egalitarianism. It abolished the remnants of feudalism, asserting the principle of equality before the law. Every French citizen, regardless of their status or wealth, was subject to the same laws. The Code recognized the sanctity of private property, allowing individuals the freedom to use, dispose of, and inherit property.

The Code also played a crucial role in shaping civil relationships. It codified marriage as a secular institution, putting it firmly within the realm of civil law. It outlined the rights and obligations of spouses, the rules of divorce, and the regulations concerning the guardianship of children.

However, the Code was not without its flaws and contradictions. While it championed the principles of equality and personal freedom, it was remarkably regressive when it came to the rights of women and children. Women were given fewer rights than their male counterparts. They were deemed to be under the guardianship of their husbands, with limited property rights and no rights to divorce on the same grounds as men. Children, on the other hand, were subjected to the authority of their parents, with little rights of their own.

Despite its limitations, the Napoleonic Code's influence extended far beyond the borders of France. As Napoleon's armies marched across Europe, they carried with them this revolutionary legal code. The Code was implemented in the territories Napoleon conquered or influenced, from the banks of the Rhine to the plains of Italy, the valleys of Spain to the lands of Poland.

The Napoleonic Code's legacy in Europe is a testament to its transformative power. It served as a basis for legal systems in various European countries, contributing to the abolition of feudalism, the recognition of personal and property rights, and the establishment of a modern, rational legal order.

Even beyond Europe, the Napoleonic Code cast a long shadow. It influenced the civil law traditions of Latin America, parts of Africa, and the Middle East. It inspired the modernization of Japanese law in the 19th century and even found its way into the Louisiana Civil Code in the United States.

The Napoleonic Code, therefore, is not merely a collection of laws; it is a piece of history, a symbol of a time of profound transformation. It is a testament to the power of law as a tool of societal change and a monument to Napoleon's vision of a modern, rational society.

As we trace the lines of this remarkable legal code, we encounter the mind of Napoleon Bonaparte, the jurist. We see a man who understood the power of law, who knew that his military victories would fade, his empire might crumble, but a legal code, once embedded in the fabric of society, would endure. And endure it has.

The Napoleonic Code remains one of the enduring legacies of Napoleon Bonaparte, a testament to his vision and his impact. It is a testament to his belief in the power of law to shape society, to establish order, to ensure justice. It is a testament to a man who, in his own words, wished to be remembered not as a conqueror, but as a lawgiver. As we continue to navigate the legal landscapes shaped by the Napoleonic Code, we are reminded of Napoleon's vision, his ambition, and his enduring impact on the world.

Chapter 26:

Assessing the Man

He was more than a general, more than an emperor, more than a statesman. He was, in essence, a man. Napoleon Bonaparte - the figure whose name resounds through the annals of history, sending ripples of awe, admiration, and, quite often, reproach. But beneath the façade of the grand conqueror, beneath the robes of the ruler, who was this man?

An investigation of Napoleon's personal life, his habits, his private character, unveils a portrait more intricate than the most sophisticated piece of art, more nuanced than the grandest tale ever told. The kaleidoscope of his persona reveals a man as intriguing in his personal sphere as he was in his public life, a man whose private self was as extraordinary as his legendary public persona.

Napoleon's work ethic was legendary. For a man who wore multiple hats - general, statesman, emperor - one can only marvel at his ability to manage his time and responsibilities. He was known for his capacity to endure long hours of work, often late into the night, sacrificing sleep for the sake of duty. One could imagine him, huddled over his desk by the flickering candlelight, engrossed in reports from the battlefield, plans for administrative reforms, letters to foreign dignitaries. Such was his dedication that even during his campaigns, he would carry a mobile office - a 'campaign bureau,' as it was called - to ensure he could attend to state matters.

Napoleon's sharp intellect and voracious curiosity have been subjects of much fascination. He was an avid reader, his tastes as diverse as the extent of his empire. From Plutarch's 'Lives' to Caesar's 'Commentaries,' from Voltaire's verses to Rousseau's treatises, Napoleon devoured literature. History, philosophy, poetry, and science - he was drawn to all knowledge. As he himself once said, "Show me a family of readers, and I will show you the people who move the world." Books were his constant companions, his sources of inspiration, his refuge. They fueled his mind, shaped his perspectives, enriched his strategies.

Yet, Napoleon was not a man who lived only in the realms of intellect and power. He was a man of deep emotions, of intense passions. His relationship with Josephine de Beauharnais bears testament to this aspect of his personality. His letters to Josephine brimmed with affection, revealing a man deeply in love. "I wake filled with thoughts of you," he once wrote to her, "Your portrait and the intoxicating evening which we spent yesterday have left my senses in turmoil." Despite the political nature of their marriage and the tumultuous path it followed, Napoleon's love for Josephine remained, highlighting the depth of his emotions.

Notwithstanding his public image as the stern, decisive commander and ruler, Napoleon possessed a certain vulnerability, a sense of humor, and a profound sense of humanity. He would often disguise himself as a lower-ranked officer to interact with his soldiers, sharing their food, listening to their stories, instilling a sense of camaraderie and devotion among them. There are anecdotes of him playing with his children, his laughter echoing through the grand corridors of his palaces, revealing a playful, tender side to the stern emperor.

However, Napoleon was not without his flaws. He could be ruthless in his quest for power, disregarding the cost of his ambitions. His notorious temper was feared by friends and foes alike. His obsessive drive for control, his disdain for opposition, and his impatience with incompetence often led to harsh consequences.

Napoleon's ambition knew no bounds. He dreamed of a grand empire, of unmatched glory, of an immortal legacy. Yet, it was this very ambition that led to his downfall. His relentless pursuit of dominance, his belief in his invincibility, his disregard for the realities of the geopolitical landscape - these traits that propelled him to extraordinary heights were the same that precipitated his spectacular fall.

His was a life of paradoxes. He was a revolutionary who became an emperor, a liberator who turned into a conqueror, an outsider who became the epitome of French glory. He was a man of reason who believed in his destiny, a man of action who cherished the realm of ideas, a man of power who valued the simplicity of personal relationships.

The assessment of a man like Napoleon is no easy task. His life is a tapestry of brilliant victories and crushing defeats, of grand ambitions and severe miscalculations, of profound changes and terrible costs. One must tread carefully in this labyrinth of paradoxes, of extraordinary feats and flawed judgments.

He was a man of his time, yet he transcended it. He was molded by the Revolution, yet he shaped an era of his own. He was loved, feared, admired, and despised. He was, in every sense, a man larger than life. Yet, when stripped of his titles, his victories, his empire, he was, at his core, a man. A man of exceptional capabilities, of profound flaws, of unquenchable ambition, and of deep humanity.

In Napoleon, we find a reflection of the human condition in its most brilliant and most flawed aspects. He was an embodiment of the heights humans can reach, the depths they can fall into, the dreams they can realize, and the disasters they can bring upon themselves.

Thus, as we delve deeper into the life of Napoleon, into his triumphs and tragedies, his dreams and disillusionments, his victories and vanquishes, we are not merely studying the life of a remarkable man. We are exploring the potential and the paradoxes of human nature itself. We are grappling with the eternal questions of power and morality, ambition and responsibility, success and failure.

In the end, it is not the man Napoleon Bonaparte who fascinates us. It is the human Napoleon, in all his brilliance and folly, in all his glory and ignominy, that captivates our imagination, that challenges our understanding, that defies our judgment.

As we draw the curtains on this chapter, we do not merely close a segment of a man's life. We close a mirror to our own selves, a mirror that reflects our potential for greatness and our capacity for error, our dreams of glory and our fear of downfall, our insatiable curiosity and our inevitable ignorance.

To understand Napoleon, we must traverse the landscapes of history and humanity, power and passion, intellect and emotion, ambition and downfall. It is a journey not for the faint-hearted, for it requires us to confront the best and worst in us. But it is a journey worth undertaking, for it leads us to a greater understanding of not only Napoleon but also of ourselves and our place in the grand narrative of history.

Chapter 27:

The Posthumous Napoleon

Over two centuries since his death, Napoleon Bonaparte persists as an omnipresent figure in the collective memory of humanity, transcending the realm of history and assuming a near-mythical status. From classrooms to cafes, from scholarly seminars to popular culture, the specter of Napoleon looms large, inciting discussions, sparking debates, evoking emotions. But who is this posthumous Napoleon? How has the man evolved into the legend, the emperor into the icon? How has the perception of this complex, controversial character morphed over time? This chapter seeks to navigate the labyrinth of posthumous Napoleonic perceptions, examining how time and context have shaped our understanding of this extraordinary individual.

One might argue that the posthumous journey of Napoleon commenced even before his death. On the rocky outpost of Saint Helena, with the grandeur of his past juxtaposed against the desolation of his present, Napoleon, the master storyteller, embarked on the greatest narrative of his life - the narrative of his own legacy. Through his memoirs, through his conversations with his small coterie of loyal followers, he began the process of myth-making, portraying himself as a hero wronged, an emperor betrayed, a man of destiny denied his rightful place in history. It is on this remote island that the seeds of the Napoleonic legend were sown.

In the immediate aftermath of his death, Napoleon's image underwent a dramatic metamorphosis. The dictator turned into a martyr, the conqueror into a hero, the fallen emperor into an exiled legend. France, under the restored Bourbon monarchy, stifled the open veneration of Napoleon, transforming him into a symbol of quiet defiance, a beacon of hope in an era of disillusionment. The Napoleonic legend was further burnished by the romantic authors of the time. Victor Hugo, for instance, in his epic "Les Miserables," painted a stirring image of Napoleon, elevating him from a mere mortal to a divine force, an embodiment of the spirit of the age.

As the waves of time swept across the shores of history, the perception of Napoleon continued to evolve, driven by shifting political currents, changing cultural contexts, and advancing historical research. The late 19th and early 20th centuries witnessed a revival of Napoleonic studies, with historians delving deeper into his life, his policies, his wars. This period marked a shift from romanticizing narratives to more objective, nuanced analyses. Historians like Hippolyte Taine and Albert Sorel produced comprehensive accounts of the Napoleonic era, bringing to light the complexities of his character, the contradictions of his policies, the ambiguities of his legacy. The deification of Napoleon gave way to a more human, more fallible image of the emperor.

This was the era when Napoleon started to be perceived not merely as a man or a myth, but as an epoch, a transformative force that changed the course of history. The impact of his reforms, the scope of his empire, the audacity of his vision - these aspects began to be appreciated in a new light. Yet, simultaneously, his authoritarian rule, his militaristic ambitions, his contempt for opposition - these facets of his reign were subjected to increasing scrutiny. The image of Napoleon became a mirror in which the complexities, the ambiguities, the contradictions of the era were reflected.

The two World Wars of the 20th century had a profound impact on the perception of Napoleon. The horrors of war, the devastation of entire societies, the immense human cost - these stark realities painted the Napoleonic wars in a darker shade. Napoleon, the military genius, started to be viewed as Napoleon, the harbinger of war. The romantic image of the victorious general gave way to the sobering picture of the ruthless conqueror. Yet, in the aftermath of the wars, as Europe sought to rebuild itself, the other side of Napoleon - the reformer, the lawgiver, the modernizer - assumed prominence. His contributions to civil administration, legal systems, educational reforms - these aspects of his rule were brought into sharper focus.

In recent decades, as the world has become more interconnected, the perception of Napoleon has become more global. He is no longer confined to the European narrative but has become a part of a broader, more inclusive discourse. From Egypt to Russia, from Italy to Spain, different societies remember Napoleon in different lights. To some, he is a liberator who swept away the old order; to others, he is an invader who imposed his will on foreign lands. The perception of Napoleon has become as diverse as the lands he once ruled.

The image of Napoleon has been subjected to countless interpretations, a plethora of perspectives, a multitude of perceptions. It has evolved with the passage of time, shaped by the ebb and flow of ideas, the transformation of societies, the progression of historical research. Yet, throughout this evolution, one aspect has remained constant - the fascination with Napoleon. He continues to captivate our collective imagination, to stimulate our intellectual curiosity, to inspire awe and invite criticism.

In the end, the posthumous Napoleon is a reflection of our own perceptions, a product of our own contexts. He is a hero and a villain, a visionary and a despot, a reformer and a conqueror. He is as much a creation of our collective memory as he is a figure of history. He is as much a part of our present discourse as he is a relic of the past. He is, in every sense, a man of all ages, an emperor for all times.

This exploration of the posthumous Napoleon is not just a journey through the annals of history. It is an odyssey through the realms of perception, a voyage through the corridors of memory, a journey through the landscapes of imagination. As we traverse this intriguing terrain, we do not merely trace the posthumous journey of Napoleon. We unravel the intricate tapestry of human memory, the fascinating dynamics of perception, the enduring power of myths.

In the posthumous Napoleon, we find a mirror that reflects the ever-evolving nature of historical understanding, the perennial quest for truth, the perpetual interplay between fact and fiction. We find a testament to the timeless allure of history, the eternal fascination with extraordinary individuals, the enduring appeal of compelling narratives. We find a reminder of our own capacity for hero-worship, our own susceptibility to myths, our own search for heroes and villains in the complex narrative of history.

In the final analysis, the posthumous Napoleon is more than just an historical figure. He is a symbol, a metaphor, an idea. He is a symbol of the transformative power of individuals, a metaphor for the complexities of history, an idea that continues to provoke, to inspire, to captivate. He is a testament to the enduring power of history, the perennial allure of the past, the timeless fascination with the extraordinary.

The posthumous journey of Napoleon is, in essence, a journey through the corridors of time, a voyage across the landscapes of memory, a sojourn through the realms of imagination. It is a journey that challenges our perceptions, enriches our understanding, expands our horizons. It is a journey that, like the man it revolves around, is as fascinating as it is complex, as illuminating as it is intriguing, as timeless as it is timely.

Chapter 28:

Napoleon in Popular Culture

Every corner of the world has absorbed a measure of the cultural leviathan that is Napoleon Bonaparte. He's strutted the stage of global drama, such an impossibly vibrant character that his shadow has touched the farthest corners of human imagination. We find his mark imprinted deeply in the arts, from the lush strokes of Jacques-Louis David's brush to the intricate plotlines of Tolstoy's "War and Peace." He's been resurrected on the silver screen, shaping the way we remember the past and the myths we tell about ourselves. In the vast expanse of popular culture, Napoleon has been continually reinvented, his image molded to the times, yet ever emblematic of a sense of grandeur, ambition, and inevitably, hubris.

In the 19th century, British cartoonists eagerly seized upon the French ruler, transforming him into a puffed-up tyrant. The British, always adept at deploying satire as a weapon, used Napoleon as a potent figure for mockery. The inimitable James Gillray, with his acerbic wit, presented Napoleon as a gluttonous behemoth consuming the

European continent in his cartoon "The Plumb-pudding in Danger." Here, a caricatured Napoleon, his belly straining against his military garb, devours the world, satirizing his ceaseless hunger for territory.

In contrast, French artists tended to paint Napoleon in heroic hues. Jacques-Louis David, the quintessential painter of the Napoleonic era, depicted him crossing the Alps on horseback in his work "Napoleon at the Saint-Bernard Pass." In this dramatic rendition, Napoleon is larger than life, his steed rearing against a stormy sky as he points towards destiny. This kind of visual hagiography created the foundation of Napoleon's enduring image in popular culture.

Turn the pages of literature, and Napoleon strides into view, his persona employed as both historical figure and symbolic device. He plays a crucial role in Tolstoy's monumental "War and Peace," his ambition serving as a counterpoint to the Russian soul's stoic endurance. In Victor Hugo's "Les Misérables," Napoleon's spirit, though not directly present, pulses through the narrative, his shadow looming over the characters as a symbol of lost glory and enduring hope for a more egalitarian society.

The allure of Napoleon's saga continued into the 20th century, shaping even the new medium of film. Silent movie star Albert Dieudonné gave a vivid portrayal of Napoleon in Abel Gance's epic 1927 silent film. It was an innovative masterpiece of its time, using groundbreaking camera techniques to capture the frenetic energy of the battlefield and the theatrical intensity of Napoleon's rule. The audience could almost feel the ground rumbling under the hooves of the cavalry and see the steely determination in Napoleon's eyes.

American cinema too has had its share of Napoleonic dramas. Marlon Brando brought a raw intensity to his portrayal of Napoleon in the 1954 film "Désirée," showcasing the ruler's tempestuous relationship with his one-time fiancée Désirée Clary. In the humorous context, the 1989 film "Bill & Ted's Excellent Adventure" used Napoleon as a source of comic relief, an aloof conqueror thrust into the anarchy of a modern water park, a parody that underscores the inherent absurdity of transplanting a historical figure into the contemporary world.

Napoleon's influence isn't limited to the visual arts or narrative media. He's also left his footprint on music. Beethoven initially dedicated his 3rd Symphony, the "Eroica," to Bonaparte, seeing in him the embodiment of Enlightenment ideals. When Napoleon declared himself Emperor, however, Beethoven furiously scratched out the dedication, disappointed at his hero's fall from republican virtue to monarchical ambition.

In the digital age, Napoleon's story has been translated into an array of video games, from strategy-based "Napoleon: Total War," which allows players to control armies and emulate the Corsican's tactical genius, to "Assassin's Creed Unity," where Napoleon appears as a charismatic, though morally ambiguous, figure navigating the tumult of the French Revolution. These games invite us to step into Napoleon's shoes, wielding his power and facing his challenges in an immersive virtual experience.

In fashion, too, Napoleon's sartorial influence persists. The military-style coat, the high collar, gold braiding, and decorative epaulets – they all hark back to the Napoleonic era. Indeed, the empire-line dress, popular in women's fashion, draws its name from the French ruler's reign. Its high waistline was a staple of women's fashion in the early 19th century and remains a classic style to this day.

Perhaps the most fascinating aspect of Napoleon's place in popular culture is its elasticity, its ability to be continually reimagined and repurposed. From the hagiography of French painters to the satirical barbs of British cartoonists, from the poignant prose of Tolstoy to the silver screen's melodrama, Napoleon is both a man and a canvas onto which we project our ideas about power, ambition, and destiny. Whether lionized or lampooned, he remains a figure of endless fascination, a testament to the enduring power of his story in the human imagination. We can no more escape his cultural shadow than we can deny the indelible mark he left on the world.

Chapter 29:

Debates among Historians

Since the moment he burst onto the historical stage, Napoleon Bonaparte has been an enigma - a man who wore many hats, filled numerous roles, and lived his life with such energy, ambition, and audacity that even two centuries after his death, he continues to captivate and confound. Historians, from his contemporaries to scholars of the present day, have grappled with his complex legacy, seeking to unravel the man from the myth, the emperor from the statesman, the warrior from the lawgiver. In this effort, they have generated a discourse of such richness and diversity that it stands as a testament to Napoleon's profound and lasting influence on the fabric of human history.

The Napoleonic era was an age of transformation, and Napoleon himself was at once a catalyst, a participant, and a product of those profound changes. So many narratives have been woven around his life, and he has been interpreted and reinterpreted in myriad ways, reflecting the changing preoccupations of historical research and understanding. These debates are not simply about Napoleon himself but are also a window into the broader themes and trends of historiographical discourse.

One major theme in these debates is the interpretation of Napoleon's role in the French Revolution. Was he the child of the revolution, as he liked to portray himself, carrying forth its ideals of liberty, equality, and fraternity? Or was he its gravedigger, trampling on the hard-earned rights of the citizenry to fulfill his personal ambitions? Historians have long grappled with this question, reflecting the broader tensions between individual and collective action in history.

For some, like early 19th-century historian François Guizot, Napoleon was the man who betrayed the revolution. Guizot was critical of Napoleon's autocratic rule, viewing him as an opportunist who used the chaos of the revolution to consolidate his personal power at the expense of the people's sovereignty. This argument posits that Napoleon's self-coronation as Emperor was the final blow to the revolutionary spirit, replacing the ideal of citizen governance with the spectacle of monarchical authority.

In contrast, historians such as Louis Bergeron and Jean Tulard, prominent in the mid-to-late 20th century, argue for a more nuanced interpretation of Napoleon's relationship with the revolution. They view him as the heir and continuator of the revolution, albeit in a transformed mode. Bergeron, for example, argues that Napoleon's administrative centralization and legal reforms, epitomized by the Napoleonic Code, secured many of the revolution's gains, such as equal rights, property rights, and secularization. In this view, Napoleon's empire represents a kind of 'Revolution from above,' embedding revolutionary principles within a framework of order and stability.

Another point of contention among historians is Napoleon's impact on Europe and the wider world. Was he a destroyer or a modernizer? Did his wars bring ruin or progress to the continent? The answers to these questions hinge on one's perspective.

British historian Geoffrey Ellis represents one strand of this debate. He argues that the Napoleonic wars were devastating for Europe, causing widespread destruction and loss of life. For Ellis, Napoleon's relentless military campaigns were a form of continental imperialism that brought suffering to millions.

On the other hand, historians such as Owen Connelly and Harold Parker have emphasized the transformative aspects of Napoleon's rule in Europe. They point to his role in spreading the ideals of the French Revolution beyond France's borders, introducing modern administrative systems, rationalizing economies, and undermining old feudal structures. From this perspective, Napoleon appears less a conqueror than a catalyst for change, sowing the seeds of modern Europe in the scorched earth of his battlefields.

A third area of debate is Napoleon's personality and private life. Was he a military genius with a vision for a better society? Or was he an ego-driven tyrant, obsessed with power and glory? Again, the answers are complex and multifaceted.

Historians like Pieter Geyl and J. Christopher Herold, writing in the mid-20th century, underscore Napoleon's military genius, his ability to innovate on the battlefield and inspire his troops. They credit him with changing the face of warfare and introducing a new kind of military strategy that combined grand tactics with an understanding of politics and psychology.

However, other historians have painted a darker picture of Napoleon's character. Paul Schroeder, for example, criticizes Napoleon for his relentless ambition, arguing that he pursued personal glory without regard for the consequences, leading France and Europe into unnecessary conflicts.

Lastly, there has been a longstanding debate about whether Napoleon should be considered 'great.' To be sure, his influence on history is undeniable, but does this qualify him for greatness? Is greatness measured by influence alone, or does it require moral integrity as well?

Scholars like Andrew Roberts and Robert Doughty have argued that Napoleon's military successes, his far-reaching reforms, and his indelible impact on French and European history qualify him as a 'great' man. They stress his strategic brilliance, his administrative prowess, and his ability to reshape the map of Europe.

On the other hand, historians like Adam Zamoyski and Felix Markham question this narrative, pointing out the human cost of Napoleon's wars, his disregard for democratic principles, and his ultimate failure to establish a lasting dynasty. They suggest that 'greatness' should encompass ethical considerations, not just influence or ability.

In conclusion, the debates among historians about Napoleon Bonaparte are as diverse and multifaceted as the man himself. He continues to be a figure of fascination, admiration, and controversy, and these debates serve as a testament to his enduring relevance in the historical consciousness. As we grapple with our own epoch of change and upheaval, we would do well to continue engaging with the life and legacy of Napoleon, seeking to understand not only the man but the era he embodied and the transformations he set in motion.

Chapter 30:

Legacy of a Conqueror

Even when cloaked in the cool and measured tapestry of historical analysis, certain figures echo through the corridors of time with a resonance that is both audacious and awe-inspiring. Among these immortals of history, Napoleon Bonaparte stands as a titan, a man whose life and legacy have been woven into the very fabric of our collective understanding of the past, shaping the present, and continuing to influence the future.

The imprint of Napoleon's journey from Corsica to the throne of France, from revolutionary to Emperor, and from a dream of European unification to a chilling exile, is etched deeply into the narrative of human civilization. His influence is so pervasive and his legacy so intricate that each wave of historical interpretation, each shift in our understanding of the past, brings with it a fresh perspective, a new layer of complexity to our understanding of the man who was Napoleon.

To begin, let us cast our gaze over the landscape of modern France, a country shaped as much by the force of Napoleon's will as by the roll of its verdant hills and the flow of the Seine. He looms large over the nation he led, the country he shaped, and the people he forever changed. His political and social reforms, epitomized by the Napoleonic Code, laid the bedrock for the French state as we know it today.

Consider the administrative division of France into departments, a rational, geometric re-ordering that swept away the traditional provinces with their local loyalties and histories. The efficient, centralized bureaucracy that he established continues to shape the nature of French governance, while the Bank of France, another of his innovations, remains at the heart of the nation's economic structure.

Yet, his legacy in France extends far beyond these institutional and structural changes. Napoleon also fundamentally reshaped French identity, weaving a national narrative that celebrated French glory and unity. His use of symbols and ceremonies, from the epic splendor of his coronation to the monumental arches that grace Paris, created a sense of shared heritage, a sense of belonging to a grand and glorious nation. This weaving of narrative and memory helped to create a sense of national identity that has persisted to the present day.

Napoleon's influence is also evident in the very symbols of French nationhood. Consider the red, white, and blue tricolor flag, which he embraced as a sign of revolutionary continuity, or the national anthem, La Marseillaise, which he reintroduced. These national symbols, so closely associated with the French spirit of liberty, equality, and fraternity, were part of Napoleon's project of creating a cohesive national identity, and they continue to shape France's perception of itself.

Beyond the borders of France, the seismic reverberations of Napoleon's reign reshaped the contours of Europe. His sprawling military campaigns, though devastating, served as the conduit for the spread of French revolutionary principles across the continent. The notions of equality, secularism, and national sovereignty reverberated across European territories, shaking the foundations of the old feudal order.

In the lands under French control or influence, Napoleon's administrative and legal reforms were often implemented, bringing a measure of the revolutionary ideals of equality and rational law. The effects of these changes were far-reaching and long-lasting, sowing the seeds of modernity in many parts of Europe. The Kingdom of Italy, the Confederation of the Rhine, and other client states of the French Empire became testing grounds for these new ideas, with consequences that long outlived Napoleon's rule.

In Germany, for example, the dissolution of the old Holy Roman Empire and the re-ordering of the German states under the Napoleonic system contributed to a radical rethinking of German identity. It was a disruptive but formative experience that laid the groundwork for the eventual unification of Germany in the late 19th century.

The global reach of Napoleon's legacy is as expansive as the empire he dreamed of. The echoes of his ambitions and the consequences of his rule were felt as far away as America and Asia. Even the contours of our modern world, where the nation-state is the principal actor, can be traced back, in part, to the Napoleonic Wars and their reshaping of the international order.

For Napoleon's saga is not merely a tale of territorial conquest or political power. It's a narrative of ideas – potent, revolutionary, disruptive ideas – clashing with tradition, of innovation challenging convention, of the new order wrestling with the old. The legacy of Napoleon, then, is not only engraved in the borders of countries or the architecture of governance but in the realm of ideas, in the shared values and principles that shape our societies.

But we must also reckon with the less palatable aspects of his legacy – the cost in human lives, the autocracy, the sheer ambition that often outstripped the bounds of pragmatism. The Napoleonic Wars, with their revolutionary style of total warfare, ushered in an era of conflict on an unprecedented scale, leaving a trail of devastation across Europe.

Moreover, his imperial ambitions and his willingness to bend the principles of the Revolution to his ends have left an indelible stain on his legacy. The man who once a champion of liberty became an Emperor, the defender of the Revolution morphed into a military dictator. This dichotomy between Napoleon the liberator and Napoleon the tyrant forms a crucial part of his complex legacy.

So, we are left with a man who was a paradox, a dazzlingly brilliant and terribly flawed individual whose life's work continues to echo through the annals of time. He was both a visionary and a despot, a liberator and a conqueror, a child of the Revolution and its gravedigger. The legacy of Napoleon Bonaparte, thus, is as multifaceted and complex as the man himself. He is a man who defies easy categorization, a man whose shadows loom just as large as his accomplishments.

In this light, we see Napoleon not just as a figure of history, but as a mirror in which we can glimpse the grandeur and the tragedy of human ambition, the heights of genius and the depths of hubris. His legacy is a testament to the transformative power of a single individual and a reminder of the dangers of unchecked ambition. Napoleon's story, then, is more than just a chronicle of the past. It's a narrative that continues to shape our present and offers lessons for our future. It's a tale as timeless as ambition and as enduring as the human spirit. As long as there are nations to build and empires to dream of, the specter of Napoleon Bonaparte will continue to haunt the corridors of history, an eternal testament to the glory and the folly of man.

Beyond the Pages: Your Part in the Story

As our narrative journey through the turbulent life of Napoleon Bonaparte draws to a close, we invite you, our esteemed reader, to pause for a moment and reflect. History, after all, is a vibrant tapestry of interconnected threads, and your part in this ongoing narrative is more significant than you might think.

We have strived to bring you an engaging, illuminating, and comprehensive exploration of one of history's most influential figures. Our hope was not only to recount Napoleon's life, but also to spark thought, provoke dialogue, and perhaps even stir within you a deeper curiosity about the fascinating tapestry of human history.

If you found this journey compelling, if the exploration of Napoleon's life captivated your imagination or provided you with fresh insights, we would appreciate if you could share your thoughts with us, and more importantly, with fellow readers.

Your feedback not only enriches our work but also allows us to reach more history enthusiasts like you. It aids us in our mission to make history more accessible, engaging, and stimulating for all readers.

How You Can Help

There is a simple and effective way you can contribute. By leaving a review on Amazon, you help us reach a wider audience, thus extending the reach of this narrative beyond the pages of this book. A minute or two of your time can help us immensely, and we are deeply grateful for this small act of support.

Share Your Thoughts

We value every reader's perspective, and your review can also help guide future readers, providing them with a glimpse into the richness of the narrative journey that awaits them in these pages.

So, we invite you to take a moment, consider your impressions of this book, and kindly leave a review on Amazon. As historians, we are curators of the past, but you, as readers, are the vital conduits through which history is kept alive.

Thank you for joining us on this journey. The legacy of Napoleon Bonaparte echoes through time, and by reading and reflecting upon his life, you have become a part of that legacy.

Printed in Great Britain
by Amazon